Reading as a Philosophical Practice

Reading as a Philosophical Practice

Robert Piercey

ANTHEM PRESS

Anthem Press
An imprint of Wimbledon Publishing Company
www.anthempress.com

This edition first published in UK and USA 2022
by ANTHEM PRESS
75–76 Blackfriars Road, London SE1 8HA, UK
or PO Box 9779, London SW19 7ZG, UK
and
244 Madison Ave #116, New York, NY 10016, USA

First published in the UK and USA by Anthem Press in 2021

Copyright © Robert Piercey 2022

The author asserts the moral right to be identified as the author of this work.

All rights reserved. Without limiting the rights under copyright reserved above, no part of this publication may be reproduced, stored or introduced into a retrieval system, or transmitted, in any form or by any means (electronic, mechanical, photocopying, recording or otherwise), without the prior written permission of both the copyright owner and the above publisher of this book.

British Library Cataloguing-in-Publication Data
A catalogue record for this book is available from the British Library.

ISBN-13: 978-1-83998-543-0 (Pbk)
ISBN-10: 1-83998-543-7 (Pbk)

Cover Image: The Annunciation, Hans Memling.
Gift of J. Pierpont Morgan, 1917. The Metropolitan Museum of Art.

This title is also available as an e-book.

For Peter T. Norman,
uncommon reader

CONTENTS

Acknowledgements   ix

1. Philosophizing about Reading: The Very Idea   1
   Reading Matters   1
   Reading as a Philosophical Activity   3
   Haven't I Read This Story Before?   7
   Fanfare for the Common Reader   8
   Two Objections   10

2. The Reading Self   15
   Lost in a Book   15
   Describing the Act of Reading   19
   Further Steps   22

3. The Reading Life   27
   About a Boy   27
   What to Read   29
   Rereading   32
   How to Feel about Oneself as a Reader   34
   Stories and Quests   36

4. Ethics *from* Reading?   41
   Improving Reading   41
   The Supply-Side Approach   43
   The Conversational Approach   47
   A Hermeneutical Approach   49
   Where This Leaves Us   53

5. Ethics *of* Reading?   57
   Responsible Readers   57
   Two Kinds of Responsibilities   59
   A Deontological Approach   61
   An Alterior Approach   63
   A Eudaimonistic Approach   65
   Practices, Traditions and History   67

6.	Reading Things	71
	Here's the Thing	71
	Relating to Books	74
	Collecting the Virtual	81
	Collecting Writ Large	85
	Collecting the Collectors	88
7.	The Future of the Common Reader	91
	A Digital Future?	91
	Changing Practices	92
	Changing the Questions	96
	Changing Philosophy	99

Notes	105
Bibliography	121
Index	127

ACKNOWLEDGEMENTS

This book has been in the works for a long time, and I've received a lot of help while writing it. First and foremost, I'm grateful to everyone at Anthem for helping to bring the project to press. Megan Greiving and Elle Bloomberg gave expert editorial guidance at every stage of production. Philip Davis and Rafe McGregor made careful and thoughtful comments on the entire manuscript, and the book is much stronger as a result of their suggestions. Needless to say, any remaining mistakes are mine alone.

Some of the material from Chapter 2 originally appeared in *Philosophy in the Contemporary World* (vol. 18), and an early version of Chapter 5 was published in *Philosophy Today* (vol. 54). I'm grateful to these publications for allowing me to reuse this material here. In addition, parts of the book were presented to audiences at Memorial University, Mary Immaculate College of the University of Limerick, University College Cork and at annual meetings of the Society for Ricoeur Studies. I'm grateful to all of these audiences for their comments and criticisms.

Many, many people discussed the subject matter of this book with me and offered feedback, advice and encouragement. I'm grateful to all of them, but I'd like to single out Alicia Finch, Patrick Gamez, Leanne Groeneveld, Matt Halteman, Joel Hubick, Morny Joy, Chris Lawn, Todd Mei, Alex Obrigewitsch, John Scott and Steve Watson. Jan Purnis deserves special thanks for her unflagging interest in the project. Anna Mudde deserves extra-special thanks for, well, everything.

Chapter 1

PHILOSOPHIZING ABOUT READING: THE VERY IDEA

Reading Matters

Why do people care so much about reading?

This sounds like a silly question. *Of course* people care about reading. They care about it because it's important, and what's more, we have a pretty good idea of *why* it's important. Reading well is an important skill, one that is all but indispensable in contemporary knowledge economies. An interest in reading correlates strongly with career success: studies show that the habit of reading for pleasure in adolescence is "associated with a significantly improved percentage of entering a professional or managerial job."[1] Recent research is shedding light on why. Psychologists have discovered that reading fiction sharpens the ability to interpret other people's moods and attitudes, an ability with obvious value in the workplace.[2] Reading also seems politically important. It seems plausible that people who are in the habit of reading critically are likely to be better informed citizens than those who do not, and for this reason, Paulo Freire calls reading a "clearly political practice."[3] Finally, of course, reading is a source of great enjoyment for many people. Though there is some evidence that reading is on the decline—a 2018 study by the US Bureau of Labour Statistics found that the number of Americans reading for pleasure fell by roughly 30 percent since 2004[4]—other studies offer a rosier view. The National Endowment for the Arts, for instance, has found that the number of Americans reading for pleasure actually rose significantly from 2002 to 2008.[5] In any case, no one can deny that those who *do* read for pleasure are more enthusiastic and more visible than ever. Signs of their enthusiasm—from the popularity of celebrity book clubs to "mass reading events"[6] such as *Canada Reads* and *Read Across America*—are everywhere. Given all this, it seems silly to ask why people care about reading. Reading is an invaluable tool with clear practical benefits.

But is this a good answer? The practical benefits of reading may explain why people care about reading *at all*. But they don't explain *how much* many people care about it, or the precise *ways* in which they care about it. To many people, reading isn't just a useful tool, and reading well isn't the same sort of skill as driving well or being able to operate one's smartphone. It seems to have some deeper value. Similarly, many people who read for pleasure don't see it as just one pleasure among others, on a par with drinking wine or playing video games. They see it as a different kind of pleasure: not just more intense than other pleasures, but qualitatively different, and important for a different and more profound sort of reason. Pierre Bayard exaggerates only a little when he says that we "live in a society […] where reading remains the object of a kind of worship."[7] Consider the differences between the ways we talk about reading and the ways we talk about other skills. Few people would expect a high school math class to instill in students a love of trigonometry, one they will have for the rest of their lives and pursue in their free time. But it's quite common for people to claim that education should instill in students a lifelong love of reading.[8] Many of reading's advocates go further still. Harold Bloom calls reading "the most healing of pleasures," as well as "one of the great pleasures that solitude can afford you."[9] Mark Edmundson calls it "an act of self-discovery" in which "the reader learns the language of herself."[10] Novelist Jonathan Franzen says that reading is a way of "preserving individuality and complexity in a noisy and distracting mass culture"—a way of learning "how to be alone."[11]

Nor is this view of reading confined to educators, belletristic novelists and literary critics. It is much more widespread, and anyone who doubts this need only look at the flood of recent books about reading. There are earnest memoirs about bookish children (*The Child That Books Built*) and adults (*Books: A Memoir*). There are long tomes, sometimes lavishly illustrated, about book collecting and the adventures of those who engage in it (*A Splendor of Letters, Patience and Fortitude*). There are stories about those whose passion for books led them to despair or criminality (*The Man Who Loved Books Too Much*). There are scientific studies of the physiology of reading (*Proust and the Squid, Reading in the Brain*). There are books that advise us on how to read (*How to Read and Why, How to Read Literature Like a Professor*). And there are self-help manuals inspired by specific authors, books that explain *How Proust Can Change Your Life, What Jane Austen Taught Me about Love and Romance* and *Why You Should Read Kafka before You Waste Your Life*. To be sure, some of these books are ambivalent about the value of the reading life. Nicholas Basbane's accounts of book collecting call it a form of madness—albeit a "gentle" one—and Lynne Schwartz claims to have been *Ruined by Reading*. Usually, though, this ambivalence is at least a little tongue-in-cheek, and it only underlines how much reading matters to these authors. Reading, they suggest, matters so much, and in such profound ways, that it's *worth* going mad for. It's worth ruining one's life.

Why? Why does reading matter so much to so many people? This book is an attempt to answer that question. The view I'll be advancing is that one of the reasons reading matters to people is that it's a philosophical activity. For many of us, I'll argue, reading offers a way of reflecting on philosophical matters, a way of posing, and perhaps taking a stand on, philosophical questions. By "philosophical question," I don't just mean the kind of question that gets discussed in university philosophy departments. I don't just have in mind the kind of explicit theorizing found in seminar rooms and journal articles. I mean something related, but broader: a kind of reflection on experiences and capacities that are distinctive to human beings. As I see it, this reflection has much the same aim as the discussions found in philosophy seminars and journals. It can even have a similar result, leading those who engage in it to adopt views on certain issues. But it's usually not as explicit or as self-aware. It might seem strange to use the term "philosophy" to refer to something so fuzzy. But there is plenty of precedent for doing so. Stephen Mulhall speaks in very similar terms when he says that films can themselves be pieces of philosophy.[12] So do many of the thinkers who have claimed, over the centuries, that religion has a philosophical dimension. Film and religion aren't identical with philosophy, but people who engage with them often have the sense that they're doing something that could also be done in a more explicitly philosophical mode: reflecting on, and perhaps learning something about, a certain kind of distinctive, fundamental question. They may not be fully aware that they're doing so, and they may not reach any definitive conclusions as a result of their efforts. But neither of these facts prevents an activity from being philosophical. Reading, I'll argue, is philosophical in just this way—in the way film and religion can be.

Note that I've been speaking about the *activity* of reading—not about *what* we read. I'm not just claiming that reading is philosophical on those occasions when we read the writings of philosophers, or pieces of fiction with clear philosophical content. I'm claiming that there's something about the *activity* of reading, and the experiences people have while engaging in it, that is philosophical. Reading's philosophical side is not only, and not mainly, a function of what we happen to be reading. It has to do with the activity of reading itself.

Reading as a Philosophical Activity

I've said that the act of reading is a way of reflecting on philosophical questions. But what is a philosophical question? Obviously, this is an enormous issue, and I won't try to settle it here. But for the sake of fixing ideas, we might say that philosophical questions are ones that reflect on certain distinctively human capacities: acquiring knowledge, having moral values, experiencing beauty and the like. Often, philosophical questions reflect on the presuppositions of these capacities, or on the tensions that these capacities involve: how is knowledge different from mere true belief? How should we address conflicts between our duties to others and to ourselves? Are there objective standards of beauty? This characterization is very loose, and deliberately so, because I'd like to leave as open as I can the difficult question of what philosophy is. In particular, I'd like to leave open the question of whether philosophy has anything like a fixed nature. It's certainly possible to think that it does—to think, in other words, that certain questions and not others are the truly philosophical ones, questions so basic and so important that all thinkers ought to raise them sooner or later. At the other extreme, it's possible to think that philosophy has no stable nature at all, and to agree with Richard Rorty that calling a question philosophical is mainly a way of saying that I consider it "so important that [it] *should* have been on the minds of thinkers of all times and all places."[13] And of course, there are many positions between these extremes. For my purposes, I don't think it's necessary to settle this issue. When I say that reading is philosophical, all I mean is that it involves reflection on issues that readers recognize as philosophical—or that they *would* recognize as philosophical, if they were asked. I want to leave open the question of what makes these issues philosophical, whether it be a fixed nature, or the mere fact that someone considers them important, or something in between. As for what these issues might be, the best I can do is offer some examples. Here are three that seem especially germane to the topic of reading.

The first is the topic of *selfhood*. This topic concerns our understanding of what we are: of what kind of beings we are, and of what it's like to be a being of that kind. In reflecting on selfhood, we might ask how the physical side of our being is related to another side, if we think there is one. We might ask whether a person remains the same being at different points in time, and if so, in virtue of what. We might ask how the being I call myself is related to other beings different from it. These are classic philosophical questions, but they're also questions closely linked to the topic of reading. At least some readers—especially the devoted ones Alan Jacobs calls "extreme readers"[14]—have had their views of selfhood powerfully shaped by their experiences of reading. Such readers would probably agree with Harold Bloom that "we read—as Bacon, Johnson, and Emerson agree—in order to strengthen the self, and to learn its authentic interests."[15] And they would probably agree with Jacobs that this sort of learning involves an *"expansion of being"*[16] that is both valuable and enjoyable. Again, I don't mean that they have necessarily read explicit philosophical discussions of these topics. I mean that their experiences of reading have powerfully shaped their sense of what they are and of what it's like to be that sort of thing.

A second set of questions are *ethical* ones: questions about how to live. Such questions can focus quite narrowly on the rightness or wrongness of certain actions, or on the proper responses to certain conflicts or dilemmas. They can also deal quite broadly with what a good life is and how it is best attained. Regardless, serious readers often report having had their ethical views shaped by their experiences of reading. They may report having reached certain ethical views partially as a result of their reading. In particular, they sometimes sense that reading has helped to develop in them capacities that are ethically important, such as a tolerance for complexity or an empathy for other people. Conversely, they might suspect that reading has had ethically negative effects on them, making them less engaged with the public sphere or less sensitive to the sufferings of others. And they might be particularly interested in the ethical considerations they take to govern reading itself—that is, in the question of what it means to read well. Regardless of the form their interest takes, serious readers are unlikely to see reading as ethically neutral. They are likely to view their activity as some sort of "moral laboratory."[17]

A third set of questions are *ontological* ones: questions about which things exist and what those things are like. Ontological reflection can be quite general, as when it looks for an overall theory of what sorts of things exist. It can also reflect on the categories or concepts we can use to understand those things, or help clarify the meanings that certain things have for us. These questions, like questions about selfhood or ethical matters, have clear links to the topic of reading. For some extreme readers, reading is a particularly instructive way of reflecting on the nature of things, and on the nature of their relations with things. Readers often care a great deal about collecting physical copies of the books that matter to them. Walter Benjamin famously saw an ontology in this urge: an attempt to relate to things simply as things, "a relationship to objects which does not emphasize their functional, utilitarian value."[18] A different but related ontology seems to be at work in those readers who like to accumulate *readings*—who read a book, in part, for the satisfaction of having finished it. To some readers, the experience of reading is an important way of reflecting on things and thinghood.

In short, reading is philosophical in that many people experience it as a way of reflecting on classic philosophical questions—on matters of selfhood, ethics and ontology. But it's also linked with philosophy in another sense. While readers often have the sense that they're learning something about philosophical topics as they read, *what* they claim to be learning is unclear, or paradoxical, or full of tensions. Reading seems to offer lessons on philosophical topics, but those lessons often cry out for clarification. Consider the sorts of things extreme readers say when describing their experiences or explaining why reading matters to them. A common claim is that reading is an intensely private activity. It involves, we are told, a special sort of turn inward, a movement away from everyday preoccupations and ways of relating to others. As we've seen, Jonathan Franzen describes reading as a way of learning "how to be alone."[19] At the same time, readers often describe this turn inward as a way of making contact with others, a way of joining communities quite different from the ones in which they spend most of their time. To quote Franzen again, reading "both feeds on a sense of isolation and aggravates it. […] [A]t some point [readers] begin to feel a gnawing, almost remorseful need to be alone and do some reading—to reconnect to that community."[20] Consider as well the things readers say about the imagined worlds encountered while reading, particularly while reading works of fiction. Reading's appeal has much to do with escape—with the fact that what one reads is an illusion or a projection and is acknowledged as such. Yet we often condemn as philistines readers who are not moved by these illusions and projections, who do not suffer agonies of suspense while awaiting the resolution of a well-constructed plot. Readers can therefore hold opposed attitudes toward the reality of what they read, and hold them simultaneously. And there are many such paradoxes. Michael Benton argues that reading is paradoxical in at least ten respects, though he restricts himself—needlessly, I think—to the reading of fiction. He points out that reading is at once active and passive, involving "both constructive and receptive elements."[21] The reader "both *makes* things happen and *lets* things happen."[22] She subordinates herself to the voice of the text, letting herself be pulled along by the flow of a story or the logic of an argument. But she also actively reworks the text, concretizing it in her imagination and filling in its "places of indeterminacy."[23] Benton further argues that there is something paradoxical about the way readers experience time. Reading is at once "anticipatory yet retrospective."[24] Making sense of any particular point in the text involves retaining what has been read so far. But as Benton points out, "the main thrust of the *engrossed* reader […] is forwards, anticipating what is to come."[25] To read is to preserve what is past while ceaselessly turning away from it.

These paradoxes may be only apparent. We may be able to dispel them by drawing distinctions, clarifying our terms, and carefully thinking them through. The point is simply that there *is* something to think through here. Though it's common for readers to experience their activity as a way of reflecting on philosophical matters, it's much less common for them to sort out the confused results of these reflections. As Andrew Piper puts it— perhaps a tad hyperbolically—"we really have no idea what it is people do when they read. That is one of reading's great gifts to ourselves—the creation of a practice that is fundamentally opaque."[26] In short, reading is not just philosophically significant. It also stands in need of philosophical clarification.

It calls out for the kind of active, explicit investigating found in journals and seminar rooms.

Haven't I Read This Story Before?

But why do we need a *new* investigation of reading? Haven't philosophers been talking about reading for the entire history of philosophy? Plato's *Phaedrus* is a classic discussion of the dangers of encountering ideas in writing rather than through face-to-face discussion. Descartes spent quite a bit of time reflecting on the "great advantage" and "considerable danger" involved in reading the works of earlier thinkers.[27] According to John Russon, Hegel takes reading as a model for all acts of the understanding, claiming that we "read" the world every time we try to "discern the sense expressed through some manifold determinacy."[28] French philosophy of the past 50 years sometimes seems to talk about little *but* texts and reading. Given all this attention, what could remain for philosophers to say about reading?

It's certainly true that the history of philosophy contains many discussions of reading, and of the problems and puzzles associated with it. But what's striking about these discussions—at least to me—is how little they have to do with the kinds of reading that are most familiar to most people. I have in mind here simple, everyday reading for pleasure, the kind of reading we do when we pick up a novel or biography for enjoyment or distraction.[29] The idea of reading for pleasure is a fuzzy one, and it's hard to draw a line between reading for pleasure and other kinds of reading. But in many cases, the kinds of reading studied by philosophers are noticeably different from the kinds of reading that matters most to extreme readers. The kind of reading that Bloom calls "the most healing of pleasures"[30] seems quite different from Russon's attempts to "discern the sense expressed through some manifold determinacy."[31] To the extent that philosophical discussions of reading focus more on the latter than on the former, they are likely to be out of step with the kind of reading that matters so much to so many people.

In fact—and this is a big generalization—many philosophical studies of reading don't really discuss *reading* at all. Instead, they focus on other phenomena that are tied to reading, but distinct from it.[32] Some are concerned with what comes *before* the act of reading: the conditions that are presupposed whenever we read. These are the sorts of discussions associated with deconstruction and hermeneutics, for example: attempts to show that reading is conditioned by the play of difference, or the movement of tradition, or some other condition.[33] Other discussions are concerned, roughly speaking, with what comes *after* reading: with the effects reading has on other activities, or with the implications that reading has for other topics. This category includes discussions of the effects reading has on the ability to philosophize,[34] or moral development,[35] or the emotions.[36] I don't want to dismiss work of this sort, or deny that it has valuable things to offer a philosophical study of reading. On the contrary, as I proceed, I'll often draw on ideas and insights from work of this sort. But for the most part, this body of work doesn't focus on what interests me: the activity of reading *itself*, considered as a way of engaging with philosophical questions. And work of this sort is particularly silent about the version of this activity that is most familiar to most people: ordinary reading for pleasure. So although much work already exists, there is still much for philosophy to do.

If we want to understand reading—the kind that matters deeply to large numbers of people—we need to approach it differently. We need to study reading philosophically, but we can't just build on academic work that analyzes what precedes it or follows it. We need to focus on reading in itself and as such, reading as it's experienced by all those who find it philosophically significant, but who may not fully understand why. How can we bring this sort of reading into view?

Fanfare for the Common Reader

Virginia Woolf's essay "The Common Reader" suggests a strategy.[37] Woolf, of course, was a great reader, and the essays collected in the two series of her *Common Reader* are models of sensitive, thoughtful reading. But Woolf sketches an approach to reading that is starkly different from the ones found in most academic discussions of the topic. Borrowing a term from Samuel Johnson, Woolf speaks of the "common readers" who inhabit "all those rooms, too humble to be called libraries, yet full of books, where the pursuit of reading is carried on by private people."[38] The common reader, Woolf tells us,

> differs from the critic and the scholar. He is worse educated, and nature has not gifted him so generously. He reads for his own pleasure rather than to impart knowledge or correct the opinions of others. Above all, he is guided by an instinct to create for himself, out of whatever odds and ends he may come by, some kind of whole—a portrait of a man, a sketch of an age, a theory of the art of writing. He never ceases, as he reads, to run up some rickety and ramshackle fabric which shall give him the temporary satisfaction of looking sufficiently like the real object to allow of affection, laughter, and argument.[39]

This dense passage identifies several features of the common reader. First, the common reader "reads for his own pleasure" rather than for professional reasons. Woolf contrasts this pursuit of pleasure with the work of scholars and critics, suggesting that it's valued for reasons other than pedantry and professional advancement. His motives, Woolf suggests, are not fully clear to him; his reading is "guided by an instinct." Nevertheless, the enjoyment sought by the common reader is not thoughtless or unreflective, and it is not entirely different from the work of critics or the sphere of high culture. Like the critic, the common reader is driven by a desire to understand what he reads. He is also driven by a desire to put his reading to use, by making it "serve his purpose" and "round his structure."[40] The common reader seeks understanding, but a different sort of understanding than that prized by critics and scholars.

Woolf calls this sort of understanding an "understanding of the whole," and she is vague about what it involves. But a recurring theme of her discussion is a concern with whole *persons*—with a kind of understanding that integrates the different sides of the reader's being. For one thing, she is attentive to the ways in which the common reader's pursuit extends over time. She doesn't focus here on single episodes or reading, or on isolated texts. She calls reading "a pursuit which devours a great deal of time,"[41] as well as one that is "guided by an instinct," a mission, a goal. Moreover, the common reader seeks to satisfy the emotional and affective sides of his being, not just the narrowly intellectual ones. The satisfaction he strives for involves "affection" and "laughter" as well as "argument." These sides of his being are not cordoned off from his search for understanding, but instead feed it. The common reader also seeks to integrate different kinds of reading and reading material. There isn't just one kind of reading that will help him "run up [his] rickety and ramshackle fabric." He is willing to use anything and everything, "snatching now this poem, now this scrap of old furniture, without caring where he finds it or of what nature it may be."[42] The common reader seeks to integrate his reading with the circumstances in which it takes place—especially the material circumstances. Woolf notes that his reading takes place in rooms "too humble to be called libraries," and she notes that he is "worse educated" than the scholar, and less "gifted." Her reference to "*all those* rooms" in which private people read implies that common readers form a virtual community, and perhaps that they recognize themselves as belonging to this community. Every common reader is thus a product of a biographical, social and economic context, and his reading expresses those contexts. In short, the common reader is someone who reads as a whole person. He has intellectual goals, but not narrowly instrumental ones. Through his reading, he seeks to become a certain kind of person, to lead a certain kind of existence. His reading grows out of this search, gives it expression and continually shapes it. The common reader is not just someone who reads, but someone who leads a *reading life*.

I've lingered over Woolf's discussion because it offers some valuable hints about how to study reading. My goal in this book is to examine the experiences of the common reader. I won't just examine the kinds of reading that academics engage in. Instead, I'll focus on the kinds of reading that are most familiar to most people—everyday reading for pleasure—and on the experiences people have while engaged in it. I'll pay special attention to the puzzles and paradoxes involved in these experiences, and I'll use the tools of academic philosophy to try to sort out some of these puzzles and paradoxes. In all of this, however, I won't assume that everyday reading for pleasure is thoughtless, or unreflective, or completely opposed to professional criticism. On the contrary, I'll treat it as, in part, a kind of philosophy: a way of reflecting on certain distinctively human experiences and capacities. But I'll try to understand this reflection holistically. I'll approach it as something that's done by whole persons—persons with bodies, emotions, projects and histories. I'll also treat it as something that is done in specific biographical, social and economic contexts, and that is inescapably shaped by this fact. To focus on the common reader, then, is to treat reading as something that is multifaceted, embedded and embodied.

Two Objections

I've said that I plan to focus on the experiences of common readers. But the word "experience" makes some philosophers nervous. For one thing, to speak of *the* experiences of readers, or of reading *in itself and as such*, might suggest that reading has a fixed essence. It might suggest that there are features displayed by every single act of reading, and that it's possible for philosophers to identify them. It might even suggest that the essence of reading is timeless or transcultural, or that philosophers have some special power to identify essences that others do not. If I were saying any of things, they would certainly be problematic. There are many different kinds of reading, and many different kinds of experiences associated with them. No doubt reading plays radically different roles, and involves radically different experiences, in different cultures. A culture in which silent reading is the norm will generate very different experiences than one in which it is normal to read aloud. A culture that reads mostly texts printed on paper will foster very different experiences than one in which texts are mainly encountered on electronic screens. For all these reasons, it is unhelpful to proceed as though reading has a timeless, universal essence, or to look for features that every act of reading would have to display. But there is a danger of going too far in the other direction. Though we shouldn't assume that all experiences of reading are the same, neither should we assume that they have nothing in common, or that there is nothing general to be said about them. Sheer uniformity and total diversity are not the only options. There is a useful parallel here with the ways philosophers understand selves. Selves display a certain identity over time. I am, presumably, the same person I was a day ago, or a year ago. But the identity of a self is not that of a static thing. It is a more subtle kind of identity, a kind compatible with significant diversity and change. Similarly, it makes sense to speak of a single activity called reading, and a single set of experiences called experiences of reading, even if instances of this activity and these experiences vary a great deal.

In order to make sense of reading's identity, without claiming that it has a single essence, I'll often speak of it as a *practice*. I borrow this term from Alasdair MacIntyre, who uses it to refer to

> any coherent and complex form of socially established cooperative human activity through which goods internal to that form of activity are realized in the course of trying to achieve those standards of excellence which are appropriate to, and partially definitive of, that form of activity.[43]

There's a lot in this definition, but I'd like to focus on just a few of its features. First, practices are *social*. A single person can't sustain a practice on her own. Even if the activities that make up a practice are largely solitary—like the activity of reading—the practice itself is more than the solitary acts. It is a large-scale, long-term undertaking that individuals contribute to but don't fully control. Second, practices are *structured*. Their participants can't carry them out in just any way they please. A chess player is not free to continue playing after his king has been mated, and a football team is not free to retain possession of the ball right after losing a fumble. Such constraints follow from the goals that practices pursue. We take part in a practice because we seek certain goods, and if we wish to attain these goods, we have to behave in some ways rather than others. Finally, practices are *mutable*, though not entirely lacking in unity. Chess and football both have long histories, and at various points in those histories, their rules have changed. But at any given point in its history, most of a practice's rules have to remain static. A football league can tweak its rules at the end of the season, but a quarterback can't unilaterally change the rules governing turnovers right after he's thrown an interception.

The crucial point about practices is that while they don't have essences—they change too much, and none of their features are immune to revision—they still display considerable continuity. At any given point in a practice's history, there is a great deal of uniformity in the way people participate in it, and in the experiences they have while doing so. This uniformity stems from the goals of the practice—or from the "goods internal to that form of activity," as MacIntyre puts it. In what follows, I will often speak of reading as a practice. I will do this to emphasize that experiences of reading display some identity over time, but not the identity associated with a fixed essence. It follows that we can make some general claims about the experience of reading, even if these claims don't try to identify the necessary and sufficient conditions met by all acts of reading everywhere.

Another advantage of calling reading a practice is that it helps remind us that reading is not just a single act, but a complex cluster of activities. In particular, it helps remind us that reading is more than simply casting one's eyes over a page or a screen. When some people hear the word "reading," this is what they think of: moving one's eyes over words and decoding their meanings. Similarly, when psychologists say that they're using eye scanners to study reading, this is the process they seem to have in mind. But when common readers reflect on the ways reading matters to them, they usually have something very different in mind: something that's linked to the process of casting one's eyes over printed characters, to be sure, but that is bigger, more complex and more diffuse. For one thing, it includes many different ways of extracting sense from printed characters (and perhaps other media). It includes both the close reading of the critic and the careless skimming of the blog reader. It involves very different ways of retaining, or not retaining, what one has read: finding a book deeply meaningful, or keeping only a vague recollection of it, or forgetting that one has read it at all. Pierre Bayard's *How to Talk about Books You Haven't Read* has been widely (and unfairly) mocked for blurring the line between reading and nonreading. But Bayard is surely right when he says that "we must consider just what is meant by *reading*, a term that can refer to a variety of practices."[44] More importantly, when common readers reflect on the ways in which reading matters to them, they have in mind many different activities, and the time they spend casting their eyes over a page is only one part of them. There are decisions about what to read and how: should I start *Moby Dick* again even though Melville has never really grabbed me? How much of an effort do I owe this book? How far should I read before I toss it aside again? There are decisions about the different goals I bring to my reading: how much of my reading should be devoted to sheer entertainment, and how much (if any) to books that I hope will edify me? How much to fiction and how much to nonfiction? There are decisions about rereading: would it be better for me to spend my vacation with some classic I've never opened, or rereading a beloved book I've already read twice? How many times can I reread the old favourite before it starts to lose its charm? How many more books can I expect to get through before I die, and what, if anything, should I do about that? And there are questions about the effect reading has on my character: should I feel guilty about enjoying *Lolita*? Would it be better to avoid *American Psycho* altogether? When I say that I want to understand the experiences of readers, I have in mind much more than the act of casting eyes over printed characters. I mean the experience of *leading a reading life*: the many decisions, acts and experiences that go into living a life in which reading matters to us. That is one of the reasons it will be helpful to think of reading as a practice—as a complex cluster of activities that change over time, that involve interactions with others, and that can be done well or done badly.

A second objection to focusing on the experiences of readers is that experiences seem to be private and incommunicable. You seem to have no direct access to my experiences, and I seem to have no direct access to yours. We might therefore worry that experiences are too fuzzy and obscure to be of use in a philosophical study of anything. We might think that a philosophical study of reading should focus something publicly observable: texts, or empirical observations, or the logical structure of language. Otherwise, we risk making claims that cannot be verified, or that lack any clear meaning at all. To some extent, I simply reject this criticism. I don't think the notion of experience is always as fuzzy as some philosophers claim, and I don't think it can always be replaced without loss in philosophical investigations. I suspect that in many cases, experiences are precisely what philosophers *need* to focus on—although demonstrating this would be a large undertaking. But I agree that the private character of experiences is problematic. If we want to study the experiences of readers, we can't simply marshal these experiences themselves and examine their features. We have to proceed indirectly, by studying something that manifests or expresses the experiences in question. My strategy will be to focus on the *reports* of common readers: documents in which they describe their experiences and try to come to terms with them. In the rest of the book, therefore, I'll pay quite a bit of attention to what writers have said about reading, in light of their own experiences with it. I'll pay special attention to a literary genre I've already mentioned: books about books, especially books written by Jacobs's "extreme readers." Naturally, I won't stop there. I'll treat these texts as windows onto certain kinds of experiences, and I'll have things to say about those experiences that go beyond what the texts say. But the documents are where I will start. In a way, then, this book is an exercise in the phenomenology of reading: an attempt to describe, as faithfully as possible, acts of reading and the experiences they provoke. But it will be what we might call a hermeneutical phenomenology: a phenomenology that's mediated by encounters with written texts.

A consequence of this approach is that I'll pay a lot of attention to a relatively small subset of common readers: those who write about their experiences. This strategy is risky, since these authors may be different from other common readers, and their concern with writing may lead them to describe their reading in unrepresentative ways. Though there's no guarantee that these authors won't distort their experiences, there's also no particular reason to assume that they will. I have a hunch that living a reading life and writing about one's experiences as a reader are two aspects of a single thing: the activity of making experience intelligible by bringing it to language. Being a reader is one way of linguistically lighting up the world; writing about what it is to be a reader is another. Far from being at odds with each other, these activities seem to share a deep affinity. At any rate, the only way to know whether writing about these experiences distorts them is to look. We must look at particular reports by particular authors and see how successful they seem to be. We must ask whether they ring true for us, whether they shed light on experiences that would otherwise be opaque and whether they open up fruitful new lines of inquiry. The only way to know how the story ends is to follow it where it leads.

Chapter 2

THE READING SELF

Lost in a Book

In her memoir *Ex Libris*, Anne Fadiman tells the following story:

> When the Irish novelist John McGahern was a child, his sisters unlaced and removed one of his shoes while he was reading. He did not stir. They placed a straw hat on his head. No response. Only when they took away the wooden chair on which he was sitting did he, as he puts it, "wake out of the book."
>
> "Wake" is just the right verb, because there is a certain kind of child who awakens from a book as from an abyssal sleep, swimming heavily up through layers of consciousness toward a reality that seems less real than the dream-state that has been left behind.[1]

We've all heard stories like this one: stories about passionate readers getting lost in their books. These readers become so absorbed in what they're reading that they seem to leave behind their everyday world and enter a new one, a world that's radically different but that, to them, seems more real. The experience of losing oneself in reading is a staple of memoirs of socially awkward children who don't feel at home in the shared world but who seem to access another, more compelling world through books. It's an experience that's been humourously dramatized in Jasper Fforde's comic novels about literary detective Thursday Next. In Fforde's novels, reading quite literally transports people to a different world—the BookWorld—where Miss Havisham belongs to an intelligence agency called JurisFiction and the plucky Next manages to change the ending to *Jane Eyre*. Fforde's novels are madcap comedy, of course, but they appeal to readers because they take fantastic liberties with an experience that is very real. Many common readers report that books carry them away to a different realm, and while this is obviously a clumsy metaphor, it's a way of giving voice to experiences that are hard to describe but no less powerful for that.

In the last chapter, I suggested that reading is paradoxical. It is, I claimed, a complex activity whose different features are sometimes in considerable tension with one another. Many of the most interesting and widely discussed paradoxes associated with reading concern the topics of selfhood and subjectivity. Serious readers like McGahern often report that reading profoundly alters their sense of who and what they are. Their understandings of themselves, their relations to other people and other things, their ways of living through their experiences—all of these seem to be altered in strange ways during intense bouts of reading. What's more, these changes often seem to be discoveries of something important. Common readers often report feeling as though the altered subjectivity accessed through reading is their *real* self—a self that is somehow deeper or more authentic than the version of themselves that they show the world. They may characterize this self as inhabiting a sort of private inner realm, one that is reached by turning away from everyday social life and plunging into the intensely private activity of reading. At the same time, getting in touch with this deeper self isn't experienced simply as a retreat. Often, it's experienced as a turn *away* from one sort of community that is simultaneously a turn *toward* a different sort of community: their community of fellow readers, both living and dead, both real and imagined. Curiously, the self who reads attains a kind of communion with others precisely by turning away from others.

It's easy to dismiss experiences such as these. But generations of common readers have taken them very seriously. Henry James famously said that reading a literary work of art "makes it appear to us for the time that we have lived another life—that we have had a marvelous enlargement of experience."[2] Similarly, Stanley Cavell argues that certain sorts of reading—paradigmatically, the reading of Shakespeare's greatest plays—offers "an experience of *continuous presentness*," in which the reader is detached from both past and future and forced to pay "continuous attention to what is happening at each here and now, as if everything of significance is happening at this moment."[3] And Proust calls reading "the inciter whose magic keys open to our innermost selves the doors of abodes into which we would not have known how to penetrate."[4] As strong as such claims like these are, they suggest a promising way to illustrate and test my claim that reading is a philosophical activity. Selfhood and subjectivity are quintessentially philosophical topics. Few questions have been explored more doggedly by philosophers than questions about the nature of our "innermost selves"—questions about what we most fundamentally are and how we relate to other things. If the activity of reading can be a way of exploring these questions—and James, Cavell and Proust all suggest that it can—then we have a clear example of one of the senses in which reading can be a philosophical activity.

There's another sense in which reports like these are philosophically interesting. Not only do serious readers sometimes feel as though reading has taught them something about selfhood; the things they think they have learned can look mysterious and even paradoxical. What could it mean, for example, to say that reading involves a turn inward, a retreat to some private, interior space? What sort of "space," and what sort of "retreat," are at issue here? What could it mean to say that reading involves a "marvelous enlargement of experience?" Above all, how can readers resolve the conflicts that frequently arise between the different claims they make about reading? How can reading involve *both* a turn inward *and* a movement outward—or more pointedly, a movement that reaches outward *precisely because* it is directed inward? Of course, not every claim that seems paradoxical really is so. These questions and others like them may well have answers. But the answers are not obvious. And if we're to have any hope of finding them, we must first determine what the questions mean, by clarifying, explicating and drawing careful distinctions. Clarification of this sort is one of the traditional strengths of philosophy. So the claim that reading offers special access to our innermost selves is philosophically interesting in two different senses. It's both a claim about a quintessential philosophical topic, and a problem that cries out for philosophical clarification.

Of course, there's more than one way to clarify a problem. In this case, one way would be to focus on *what* certain readers read—that is, on the texts that most often trigger responses of this sort. Cavell seems to adopt this strategy when he suggests that there's something *in* Shakespeare's greatest tragedies that provokes the experience of continuous presentness. But this strategy doesn't account for what looks like an obvious fact: that no text has the same effect on every reader, and that a book that transports one reader to a remarkable inner realm might leave another cold. It also ignores the possibility that the enlargement of experience mentioned by James might have something to do with the activity of reading itself—a possibility that, as we'll see, it's unwise to rule out of court. Yet another strategy would be to seek illumination from neuroscience. We could note that the experiences of altered subjectivity that we're discussing can be correlated with specific processes in the brain, and we could speculate that understanding these experiences is simply a matter of identifying the regions in the brain where the relevant neurological events take place. This is the strategy adopted by neuroscientists currently exploring what's called the "fiction feeling hypothesis."[5] With the help of functional magnetic resonance imaging (fMRI) scanners, these neuroscientists have concluded that texts invite readers to get lost in them by "engaging the affective empathy network" in the brain, including "the anterior insula (AI), the mid-cingulate cortex (mCC), the amygdala, the secondary somatosensory cortex and the inferior frontal gyrus."[6] There's no doubt that this sort of research has a great deal to teach us. But while neuroscience can offer a lot of information about the physical instantiations of readerly experiences, such information doesn't seem to be what's required to make sense of the musings of James, Cavell and Proust. When these writers reflect on their experiences of altered subjectivity, what's unclear is what the experiences in question *are*. We want to know what James, Cavell and Proust are *talking about* when they say that reading offers a marvelous enlargement of experience, or that it hands magic keys to our innermost selves. These are metaphors, of course—but what are they metaphors *for*? Exactly what sorts of experiences are these readers having, and what is it like to have them? Knowing what's happening in the brain during the experiences doesn't answer these questions. No doubt this is what Alan Jacobs has in mind when he quips that, when he encounters neuroscientific discussions of reading, there's always a part of him whispering, "But you're not really talking about *reading*."[7]

But other kinds of clarification are available. Notice that what's most puzzling about the reports of James, Proust and others is the claim that reading involves a peculiar and uncanny sort of experience. We don't just need to know what *causes* this experience, be it something in the brain, something in particular texts or both. We may eventually want to do that, of course, but before we can, we have to get clear on what the experience itself is: what it's like, how it differs from more mundane experiences, and how it can possibly have the paradoxical features that readers say it does. Luckily, there's a type of philosophy whose mission is to clarify experiences: phenomenology. I understand phenomenology to be not a specific doctrine, but a general philosophical current that originated in the work of Edmund Husserl in the early twentieth century.[8] Phenomenology in this loose sense attaches a great deal of importance to describing particular experiences carefully from a first-person standpoint, and it insists that doing so is a necessary prelude to theorizing about these experiences or solving the conceptual puzzles that they raise. Traditionally, phenomenologists have been less interested in activities like reading than in other kinds of experiences—paradigmatically, perceiving a physical object or judging that two and two add up to four. But there's no reason the experiences of readers can't be subject to phenomenological description. In fact, several well-known phenomenologists have done just that—Roman Ingarden[9] and Emmanuel Levinas,[10] for example. But the most developed phenomenological study of reading appears in the work of Wolfgang Iser. Accordingly, in the rest of this chapter, I'd like to turn to Iser's attempt to describe and clarify the activity of reading, in the hope that it can illuminate the experiences of altered subjectivity that common readers have long claimed to have. Iser, I think, has something indispensable to offer to the project of making philosophical sense of reading. But his approach has certain limitations, and it needs to be supplemented with a different sort of resource if it is to fulfil its promise. Toward the end of the chapter, I'll suggest that the notion of a *practice*, introduced in the last chapter, offers a promising way to do so.

Describing the Act of Reading

The goal of Iser's phenomenology of reading is to describe "what actually happens when one is reading a text."[11] This project grows out of Iser's rejection of what he calls "the classical norm of interpretation," according to which understanding a text involves unearthing "a single 'hidden' meaning" behind it.[12] Single, hidden meanings are a hard sell today; conventional wisdom has it that the meaning one finds in a text is heavily dependent on what one brings to it. If we lose faith in single hidden meanings, then the activity of reading itself acquires new interest. Iser puts it this way:

> As meaning arises out of the process of actualization, the interpreter should perhaps pay more attention to the process than to the product. His object should therefore be not to explain a work, but to reveal the conditions that bring about its various possible effects. If he clarifies the *potential* of the text, he will no longer fall into the fatal trap of trying to impose one meaning on his reader.[13]

Iser begins this descriptive project in his book *The Implied Reader*, which examines the "literary effects and responses"[14] provoked by a handful of classic novels. His studies become more general and more systematic in his later book *The Act of Reading*, which draws on Husserl to give a phenomenological description of the encounter between reader and text. Iser insists it is a genuine encounter, a "dynamic interaction"[15] in which neither pole dominates. In addition to being phenomenological, Iser's project is unapologetically transcendental. He describes reading in search of possibility conditions; he seeks "a transcendental model which makes it possible for the structured effects of literary texts"[16] to arise. These effects include several of the odd, paradoxical experiences I have mentioned. Iser asks, for example, how it's possible for readers to have the sensation of being transported away from their usual world toward a different one that seems more real. He finds it puzzling that "we often have the impression, as we read, that we are living another life."[17] He also finds it curious that living this other life can change our relation to our everyday world—that "when we put the book down—we should experience a kind of 'awakening.'"[18] In short, Iser's project is clearly philosophical. He's puzzled by the experiences readers claim to have. He wants to describe and clarify these experiences, and to that end, he studies them with the distinctive methods of phenomenology. Throughout all of this, his guiding question is transcendental: How are such experiences possible? How can reading possibly be what serious readers say it is?

Iser's answer has to do with the way texts are given to consciousness. He claims that there are two crucial differences between the way we encounter texts and the way we encounter other sorts of objects. First, in reading,

> the whole text can never be perceived at any one time. In this respect it differs from given objects, which can generally be viewed or at least conceived as a whole. The "object" of the text can only be imagined by way of different consecutive phases of reading. We always stand outside the given object, whereas we are situated inside the literary text.[19]

Many aesthetic objects—paintings and sculptures, for example—confront us as something external. We may not be able to take in all their aspects at once, or ever. But we do speak of regarding a whole painting or sculpture rather than just one of its parts. We can conceive of such objects as complete wholes because they stand over against us "out there," as it were. But the texts we read are not detached from us in this way. There is no perspective outside a text from which it may be grasped at all, let alone contemplated as a whole. Reading a text involves "a moving relationship which travels along *inside* that which it has to apprehend. This mode of grasping an object is unique to literature."[20] Iser's term for this mode of grasping is the "wandering viewpoint."[21] This phrase conveys the fact that as I read, I can never take in the whole text. I have only a series of partial views determined by where I am in the text at that moment. Reading "can only take place in phases, each of which contains aspects of the object to be constituted, but none of which can claim to be representative of it."[22] To grasp a text is to inhabit it, and we can inhabit only a little at a time.

The second difference follows from the first. Since reading takes place in phases, it's an exercise in what Iser calls "consistency-building."[23] The reader's task is to synthesize the various phases of her reading in a way that minimizes conflicts among them. Consistency-building is a search for a *Gestalt*, a coherent whole that "closes itself in proportion to the degree in which it resolves the tensions between the signs that are to be grouped."[24] The *Gestalt* that forms as I read a text doesn't dissolve all its tensions. Some texts deliberately frustrate our search for a coherent meaning. Iser goes so far as to say that most literary works are not only "full of surprising twists and turns, but indeed we *expect* it to be so—even to the extent that if there *is* a continuous flow, we will look for an ulterior motive."[25] The point is simply that reading involves a movement from part to whole, an attempt to build some sort of whole out of partial perspectives. This synthesis is "not sporadic," but "continues throughout every phase of the journey of the wandering viewpoint."[26] It typically isn't performed consciously or deliberately, but is instead an example of what Husserl calls passive synthesis. The *Gestalt*, which Iser also calls the "consistent interpretation,"[27] comes neither from the text alone nor from the reader alone. It results from the interaction of both.

In short, a text that is read differs from other objects in two key ways. The reader is inside what she reads, not set over against it; and she actively builds up what she reads by synthesizing its elements. It's the combination of the two that makes reading unique. When I listen to a piece of music, I am inside it, inhabiting some particular point within it. But the elements of the piece are given, and need not be built up by me. Conversely, when I see a cubist painting, I synthesize its elements by deciphering their sense. But I still stand outside the painting and can conceive of it as a standalone whole. Only reading forces me to build up an object *and* build it up from the inside.

Iser claims that it's the combination of these factors that gives readers the sense of living through an altered subjectivity. It is because readers inhabit an object that they simultaneously build that they can become lost in what they read, caught up in a different world. On the matter of getting lost in a text, Iser says the following:

> Through gestalt-forming, we actually participate in the text, and this means that we are caught up in the very thing we are producing. This is why we often have the impression, as we read, that we are living another life. For Henry James, this "illusion of having lived another life" was the most striking quality of narrative prose.[28]

Iser's claim is that interacting with a text—building it up from the inside— "eliminates the subject-object division essential for all perception."[29] The reason I can get lost as I read is that texts are given only through a seamless fusion of what is read and who is reading, a fusion in which it can become difficult or even impossible to distinguish which pole contributes what. The *I* can get lost in the act of reading because in a sense, this act does away with the *I*. There is only this seamless fusion of reader and read, and we often can't say where one ends and the other begins. This is an odd claim, but not an unprecedented one. There are other examples of experiences that seem to involve a blurring of the boundary between subject and object. Flow states, as described by psychology, seem to fall into this category.[30] Hans-Georg Gadamer has argued that play, especially the sorts of play that are encountered in aesthetic experience,[31] involves a blurring of the boundaries of the subject. Iser's claim is that a similar blurring takes place in the act of reading, thanks to the distinctive mode of givenness that texts display. He further argues that this mode of givenness is responsible for the sense readers have that when they stop reading, the world seems strange and different. When we read, Iser says, "we are no longer present in a reality—instead we are experiencing what can only be described as an irrealization, in the sense that we are preoccupied with something that takes us out of our own given reality."[32] When we stop reading, we experience "a kind of 'awakening.'"[33] We have briefly suspended our usual relations to objects, and when we return to them, our ties to objects seem unfamiliar and remarkable. "Suddenly," Iser says, "we find ourselves detached from our world, to which we are inextricably tied, and able to perceive it as an object."[34]

Further Steps

This chapter began with the hope that Iser's phenomenology of reading could shed some light on the experiences of altered subjectivity that serious readers claim to have. Obviously, I've given only a brief sketch of Iser's work. But I think this sketch shows that Iser's phenomenology offers a helpful way of thinking about some of the peculiar experiences of common readers. These experiences, Iser suggests, are exactly the sorts of experiences one would expect readers to have, given the nature of texts. Because of the distinctive way texts have to be given to consciousness, a certain blurring of the boundaries between reader and read is to be expected from them. This blurring is a natural result of the way readers are forced to build up texts from the inside. What's more, I suspect that Iser's discoveries about the givenness of texts could be extended to some of the other paradoxes associated with reading. They might, for instance, shed some light on the paradoxical kinds of agency that seem to be involved in reading. Perhaps readers experience their activity as both passive and active, both individual and cooperative, because they're forced to build up texts from the inside. Since readers find themselves immersed in an object that takes shape around them, it shouldn't be surprising that they find it hard to distinguish what they actively add to the text from what they passively take from it. In short, Iser offers a promising model for thinking about reading and selfhood. He offers a useful general strategy for looking at reading from a philosophical perspective, and for explaining the odd and paradoxical things it seems to show about subjectivity.

That said, Iser's model has clear limitations, and to conclude, I'd like to focus on two of them. The first concerns the kinds of texts Iser considers. Iser doesn't try to give phenomenological descriptions of every kind of reading, or even of a handful of the most important ones. He's concerned solely with one kind of reading: the reading of classic works of fiction. Neither his examples nor his phenomenological descriptions deal with nonfictional texts. This isn't unreasonable, since Iser is a literary scholar who's most interested in the reading of canonical literary works, especially classic novels. But it's important to remember that the experiences of altered subjectivity described by serious readers are triggered by all sorts of texts—not just fictional ones. Machiavelli famously had such experiences while reading the political writings of the ancients, in his study, in his pyjamas.[35] Anne Fadiman claims to have them while reading her collection of books about polar exploration.[36] George Orwell reportedly had them while reading Victorian women's magazines.[37] If we take these reports seriously—and it's hard to see why we shouldn't—then we can't attribute the odd experiences of readers to factors found only in the reading of fiction. But he does just that, and this is a serious limitation of his account.

A second limitation concerns Iser's view of the purposes of reading. Iser apparently assumes that the reader's main goal—perhaps her only goal—is to unlock the meaning of what she reads. Reading, for Iser, is the attempt to arrive at a correct and coherent interpretation of a text—again, usually a classic novel. Iser does reject the idea of "a single 'hidden' meaning"[38] behind the text. He claims that meaning arises from the interaction of text and reader and so is inherently plural. Nevertheless, the pleasure that Iser associates with reading is the pleasure of discovering what a text means. The reader he has in mind seems to be the literature professor seeking a consistent interpretation of *Tristram Shandy* or *Ulysses*—and recall that Iser defines the *Gestalt* at which reading aims as a "consistent *interpretation*."[39] But consider the sheer variety of experiences that serious readers claim to have. Some of these experiences concern the search for consistent interpretations, but many do not. Many concern emotional and other affective responses to texts. Recall Franzen's language when he speaks of the "sense of isolation" readers have, and of their "gnawing, almost remorseful need to be alone and do some reading."[40] Fadiman uses similarly charged language to describe the reader who "awakens from a book as from an abyssal sleep, swimming heavily up through layers of consciousness."[41] And Woolf, as we've seen, describes the common reader as someone "guided by an instinct to create for himself, out of whatever odds and ends he may come by, some kind of whole."[42] These are far more expansive conceptions of reading than the one found in Iser. Serious reading is not only, and perhaps not usually, an attempt to interpret texts correctly. By examining only that search and bracketing all other dimensions of reading, Iser overlooks much of what's interesting about it—as well as many of the lessons reading seems to teach about subjectivity.[43]

Now, Iser could reply—does reply, in fact—that the reason he focuses on just one sort of text and one sort of readerly response is that they are the really fundamental ones, and that all others are either derived from them or best understood by analogy with them. He says, for example, that before we can explain our "practical" and "ethical" responses to a text, we must first conduct a "detailed inspection of the processes that enable [them] to arise."[44] Before we can make sense of affective responses, we must "devise a framework in order to come to grips with them."[45] This framework turns out to be the process through which a text's meaning is generated. In other words, before we can reflect on all the things a text does to us, we must first arrive at a correct interpretation of what it means. But this reply, it seems to me, begs the question. To say that the "practical" and "ethical" effects of reading must be explained by the processes that generate meaning is to assume, without argument, that meaning-generation really is primary, other processes derivative. But that's precisely what is in question here. We can't show that affective responses are derivative by simply asserting that the process of generating meaning gives rise to them.

The point is that Iser's approach, as promising as it is, needs to be broadened. This doesn't mean that there's anything wrong in principle with the project of describing reading phenomenologically. On the contrary, as we've seen, Iser's phenomenological approach allows him to make an important discovery: that reading's mysterious features are intimately connected with the way texts are given to consciousness. But Iser's phenomenology doesn't acknowledge that there's more to reading than the search for a consistent interpretation, more to the enjoyment of a text than the satisfaction of figuring out what it means. The act of reading is a complex one that involves many different aspects—I'm tempted to say *all* aspects—of the reader's being. The phenomenology of reading must recognize this fact. Rather than describing the act of reading in isolation, it should view this act in the context of human being as a whole. This is a large requirement, but it's one that has been successfully met in other areas. Many phenomenologists have claimed that certain activities are fully intelligible only against the backdrop of a comprehensive picture of human existence. The early Heidegger's description of knowing is a good example; knowing, Heidegger claims, makes sense only when it is recognized as "a founded mode of Being-in-the-world."[46] Levinas's descriptions of language use and the search for truth make a similar claim: namely, that these activities presuppose and are made possible by the ethical relation to the other.[47] Reading could be studied in a similar way. The treatment of it need not be Heideggerian or Levinasian, whatever that might mean. But it should grant from the start that reading is—to borrow a phrase from Aaron Ridley—a "part of life."[48] We need to see reading as embedded in, and expressive of, a full range of human activities and a full picture of the human person.

I won't attempt that project here, but I will make a suggestion about how it could be started. In the last chapter, I introduced the concept of a *practice*. This concept, which I borrowed from MacIntyre, refers to any "cooperative human activity through which goods internal to that form of activity are realized in the course of trying to achieve those standards of excellence which are appropriate to, and partially definitive of, that form of activity."[49] More simply put, practice are organized activities that can be performed well or badly, and that, when performed well, allow their participants to achieve certain distinctive goods. If they are to have any chance of achieving those goods, the participants need to cultivate virtues: stable character traits that will guide them in the search for the relevant goods, and that will help them avoid the many pitfalls they will encounter along the way. To recognize an activity as a practice is, among other things, to stop seeing it as an isolated event that's fully intelligible on its own. It is to see it as, essentially, an episode in a larger story—in this case, a story about how those engaged in the activity pursued a certain good, and crucially, of how they tried to make themselves into the sorts of people who have a realistic chance of achieving that good.

What I'm suggesting is that if we want a fuller picture of the way reading lets us work through the nature of subjectivity, we should view reading as a practice. We should take seriously Woolf's suggestion that it's the search for a good—to start, the creation of "some kind of whole"—that includes the search for correct interpretations, but goes far beyond it. We should entertain the possibility that this good is available only to readers who cultivate certain traits of character—readers who self-consciously reflect on what sorts of readers they want to be, and what sorts of reading lives they want to live. Viewing reading in this way wouldn't obviate the need to think about particular acts of reading, or to describe them phenomenologically. It would still be eminently worthwhile to know what it's like for a contemporary reader to read *Tristram Shandy* or make sense of *Ulysses*. But the readers engaged in these tasks could no longer be seen as mere meaning-detectors or interpretation-builders. They'd be seen as whole people who feel and want and do, and whose particular readings make full sense only in relation to those feelings and wantings and doings. Above all, viewing reading as a practice would encourage us to see it the site for a very special sort of lesson about subjectivity. It would encourage us to see reading not just as a site where one discovers what one's innermost self is—*already* is—but as a space where one reflects on what kind of person one should become, and tries earnestly to make oneself into that kind of person.

I realize how sweeping all of this sounds. The shift that would result from seeing reading as a practice would have so many ramifications for so many areas that it's hard to say where it would take us. But a good place to start would be with one feature of practices: namely, the way they're extended in time. The attempt to make oneself into the right sort of reader is something that unfolds over a whole life, in the context of the rest of that life. So in the next chapter, I'd like to look at a concrete example of how one reader tried to make sense of his own reading life. I hope that, by doing so, we'll get a fuller sense of the ways reading can help us learn who and what we are.

Chapter 3

THE READING LIFE

About a Boy

In September 2003, novelist Nick Hornby started writing a column for the *Believer* called Stuff I've Been Reading. The column reported on his experiences as a reader: which books he had bought in the previous month, which ones he had read, what he thought about the books he had read and which books he had started but abandoned. In many ways, Stuff I've Been Reading looked like a traditional book review. Each instalment singled out titles that Hornby had especially liked and described their contents, enlivened with Hornby's distinctive wit. To be sure, some of the column's features were a little unconventional. In keeping with the *Believer* policy of allowing only "acid-free literary criticism,"[1] for instance, Hornby refrained from attacking books he didn't like, and discussed only those about which he had something good to say. Still, in 2003, a casual reader might not have noticed anything distinctive about Stuff I've Been Reading. It looked like any number of other columns about literary matters.

But as the months and years passed, Stuff I've Been Reading turned into something much more interesting. What began as a series of reports on particular books became a chronicle of Hornby's life as a reader. Christmases were celebrated; Hornby got married; London was shaken by riots; children were born. All of these events interacted with Hornby's reading in complex ways, and he wrote frankly, and sometimes movingly, about how reading did and didn't fit into the rest of his life. As the columns piled up—eventually being reprinted in a series of books—Hornby's attitude toward reading seemed to shift. In the earliest installments, he sees his reading life as structured by obligations: he thinks there are books he ought to be reading even though he doesn't really want to, authors he should feel guilty for ignoring even though he's pretty sure he won't like them. But with time, Hornby comes to reject the very idea of letting duty intrude on his reading. His tastes also shift, partly as a result of conscious steering. He grows less and less patient with certain kinds of literary fiction, and more and more willing to say so. He grows bored with his usual choices and forces himself to branch out into unfamiliar genres. All the while, Hornby offers unflinching looks at the highs and the lows of his reading life: at "the way that, when reading is going well, one book leads to another and to another, a paper trail of theme and meaning; and how, when it's going badly, when books don't stick or take."[2] The highs and lows are often in tension, and Hornby doesn't try to paper over these tensions. Instead, month by month, he tries to weave them into a coherent story—a story made all the more remarkable by the fact that he's living it.

Hornby's story about his life as a reader is especially interesting in light of one of the lessons of the last chapter. That lesson is that philosophers sometimes take reading to be simpler than it is because they view it as a free-floating act, rather than as something embedded in a life. In particular, they fail to notice the consequences of the fact that reading is a practice: a complex undertaking that changes over time but that derives a degree of continuity from the goods it pursues and the standards it must follow to attain them. However, viewing reading as a practice doesn't answer all our questions about it or dispel all its mysteries. On the contrary, it gives rise to new ones. When we view reading as a practice, it becomes clear that this practice displays considerable tensions, some of them quite hard to negotiate. There are tensions in the decisions we make about what to read and about the things we hope to accomplish by reading. We must balance the desire to read a certain book or to read in a certain way *right now* with the desire to have a certain kind of reading *life*, and with the recognition that having such a life might require us to do things we don't currently feel like doing. We must weigh the desire to reread old favourites with the urge to discover new books, authors and genres. We have to balance all of these desires with the sense that there is more to the reading life than our desires: the sense that other considerations are relevant to what and how we read. Above all, we must make some kind of sense of what we are doing as we lead reading lives: what are we trying to achieve with all this reading? What are we actually achieving? How should we feel about it? It's far from clear what would count as answers to these questions, and it's far from clear how satisfactory any such answers could be.

Stuff I've Been Reading offers an instructive look at one reader's attempts to answer these questions. It depicts Hornby's reading life as an attempt to respond to the tensions, and even the contradictions, that mark a life spent with books. It suggests that there is no hope of doing away with these tensions, but that it is still possible to accomplish something through them and to learn something from them. Hornby tries to make his experiences as a reader coherent by telling a story about them—a sprawling, multi-year, open-ended story. I want to suggest that all thoughtful readers are involved in a similar process. To live a reading life is to try to weave one's experiences as a reader into a certain kind of story, albeit a story that is usually lived rather than written. Of course, most readers don't have monthly columns. But this doesn't mean that Hornby is doing something fundamentally different than they are. He's just doing explicitly something that most readers do implicitly. That's what I'll argue, anyway.

What to Read

Apart from whether to read at all, the most basic question confronting a reader is *what* to read: which titles, out of the near infinity available, will we choose? This is a daunting question because, as Pierre Bayard puts it, "the act of picking up and opening a book masks the countergesture that occurs at the same time: the involuntary act of *not* picking up and *not* opening all the other books in the universe."[3] No one can read more than a relatively small number of books in a lifetime, so the decision to read one thing rather than another carries with it real, permanent losses. This is the sentiment behind Schopenhauer's famous remarks that "the art of *not* reading is a very important one," and that "a precondition for reading good books is not reading bad ones: for life is short."[4] From its earliest installments, decisions about what to read are at the center of Stuff I've Been Reading. Each column begins with two lists: "Books Bought" and "Books Read." Some months, there is considerable overlap between the two lists; other months, hardly any. Hornby is frank that wanting to read a book right away is only one of the motives for buying it, and only rarely is it the most important one. More commonly, he says, we buy books "because of a daydream we're having—a little fantasy about the people we might turn into one day, when our lives are different, quieter, more introspective, and when all the urgent reading, whatever that might be, has been done."[5] For Hornby, then, the problem of what to read is not solved by what he has recently bought. So how does he decide what to read? In his early columns, he hopes the process of reading itself will take care of this problem. When our reading is going well, it has a momentum of its own, and we finish one book knowing which one we'd like to start next. Once in a while, it works out this way for Hornby. His encounter with *Citizen Vince* leads him to read more books by Jess Walter; his discovery of Marilynne Robinson gives him an appetite for more of her brand of literary fiction. Hornby's life as a writer also plays a role. When he publishes his first book for young adults, he is delighted to discover the classics of the genre, as though he has stumbled on "a great and previously ignored room at the back of the bookstore that's filled with masterpieces I've never heard of."[6] And there are moments of pure serendipity. Having not read John Updike for decades, Hornby is "not quite sure why an unread copy of *Marry Me* winked at me from my bookshelves"[7]—but it turns out to be exactly what he is in the mood for.

But the strategy sometimes misfires. Though there are times when his reading carries him along and shows him what to read next, Hornby goes through periods when his reading life is indifferent, even bad. Every now and then, he says, you "hit a patch of reading that makes you feel as if you're pootling about"[8]—while you might not actually dislike the books you start, they don't grab you, and you worry that you're wasting your precious reading time. Other patches are even worse, when "your mood and the mood of the book are fighting like cats," and "you'd rather do anything than attempt the next paragraph, or reread the last one for the tenth time."[9] At times like these, Hornby is at a loss about what to read next: every book he picks up seems like the wrong one. As much as he agonizes about what to start, he agonizes even more about what to finish. In the early columns, Hornby is loath to give up on a book no matter how badly it's going. At one point he says of a book that "the last four hundred and eighteen pages nearly killed me, and I wish I were speaking figuratively."[10] At the time, Hornby finds nothing odd in this attitude. It seems perfectly natural to him to finish a book simply for the sake of finishing it. Once he has more columns under his belt, though, his attitude changes. He starts to abandon books that aren't working for him, and he urges his readers to do the same.[11] He realizes that most readers have been trained not to give up on books in this way—that "we have got it into our heads that books should be hard work, and that unless they're hard work, they're not doing us any good."[12] But he comes to think that this stubbornness is counterproductive, since "you can get very little from a book that is making you weep from the effort of reading it."[13] To stick with a book come what may is also to misunderstand the purpose of reading. The reason we hesitate to give up on books—or on certain books—is that we think reading should bring us something other than enjoyment. We may feel obliged to stick with a tedious book because it's one of the 10 or 100 or 1,001 books someone has told us we must read before we die. But Hornby decides that reading for motives other enjoyment is silly. He says that "if you don't read the classics, or the novel that won this year's Booker Prize, then *nothing bad will happen to you*; more importantly, *nothing good will happen to you if you do.*"[14]

It's hard to square this rejection of readerly duty with the rest of Hornby's columns. The idea that there are certain things he ought to be reading, even if he doesn't really want to, looms large in Hornby's life as a reader. The very first instalment of Stuff I've Been Reading describes his embarrassment at only now getting around to J. D. Salinger. ("Shouldn't I have read some of these books decades ago? *Franny and Zooey*? Jesus."[15]) Similar sentiments pop up in later columns, long after Hornby's attack on the idea of reading for duty. The attack itself is oddly different from the rest of the columns. Its tone is more shrill, as though Hornby is trying to convince himself of something he doesn't really believe. It's also less personal, and discusses larger themes—a supposed "culture war"[16] that divides all books into "the trashy and the worthwhile"[17]—that don't usually figure in Stuff I've Been Reading. More importantly, though Hornby presents himself as giving advice—read only what you want to read—this advice yields little practical guidance. How do I determine what I want to read? I can and do want many different things, including things that are incompatible. My desire to read a John Grisham novel right now can clash with my longer-term but equally real desire to finish Proust by the end of the year. I also have higher-order desires. I might be itching to reread that favourite old novel right now, but I might also yearn to be the kind of person who finds pleasure in Proust, or in John Grisham. Satisfying the latter desire might require me to suppress the former one. Hornby himself wrestles with these higher-order desires. In May 2005, he reports discovering a book about peregrine falcons, and he finds himself wishing he were "the kind of person who would buy it, read it, and learn something from it."[18] It's not exactly that he wants to read it; he wants to want to read it. Desire like this are every bit as real as a desire to read *Housekeeping* or *Citizen Vince*. Our preferences are so fickle and so tangled that telling someone to read what she wants will not get her very far.

Hornby's response to this problem is to start consciously shaping his preferences. He tries to broaden his tastes, to turn himself into someone who will find pleasure in heading things he currently doesn't. In the middle of 2005, Hornby hits on a plan to make himself read science fiction and fantasy—a genre he normally wouldn't explore "in a million years."[19] His reasoning seems sound: having grown tired of his usual taste in books, he yearns for something different. He hasn't abandoned his plan to read only what he enjoys; he just wants to make himself into a person who enjoys things he currently doesn't. For a while, the plan invigorates him. But his venture into sci-fi turns out to be grim: one column begins by saying that "even buying Iain M. Banks' *Excession* was excruciating."[20] His tastes prove to be more resistant to shaping than he'd hoped. Besides, the project of consciously shaping his preferences gives rise to new problems. As the years pass, Hornby worries that his reading choices have become too self-conscious. The reading life, he feels, ought to be largely spontaneous, without too much fretting over how and where it's going. But all this active shaping isn't very spontaneous at all. This clash between the spontaneous and the planned is perhaps the biggest tension in Hornby's reading life. As we've seen, when he dreams about the reading life he'd like to have, it's one largely devoid of conscious steering, a life in which one book leads automatically to the next. But the project of writing a column about one's reading demands a self-consciousness at odds with this dream. A critic is someone who finds it natural to talk about what he reads, someone who agrees with T. S. Eliot that criticism is as natural as breathing. Hornby seesaws between these attitudes, without ever resolving the tension in a way that satisfies him. It is with both pleasure and regret that he says that "the knowledge that I had to write something for the *Believer* at the end of each month changed my reading habits profoundly."[21]

Rereading

Another question faced by every reader is what, and whether, to reread. The urge to reread is quite deep seated. Even before they can read for themselves, children ask for their favourite stories to be read to them again and again. They are comforted by returning to familiar tales, reassured to see that the characters and plot have not changed. Adults crave this comfort too. In his classic essay "On Reading Old Books," William Hazlitt says that rereading a favourite book offers "not only [...] the pleasure of imagination and of a critical relish of the work, but the pleasures of memory added to it. It recalls the same feelings and associations which I had in first reading it, and which I can never have again in any other way."[22] In this way, the books we reread are "landmarks and guides in our journey through life."[23] As we grow older, there is a new and different pleasure to be found in rereading a book and finding that it *has* changed—or rather, that *we* have changed since our last reading of it. We don't see the same things in a given book at different points in our lives. When we reread, we often notice details that escaped our attention the first time around, and because of what has happened to us since the first reading, we can interpret a book in an entirely new way. Patricia Meyer Spacks learned this on rereading Dostoyevsky. "In a youthful reading of *Crime and Punishment*," she notes, "Raskolnikov seems a daring young man, exciting in his willingness to defy convention. As a grown-up rereader, I think him a fool, or a monster."[24] Rereading can register change as well as continuity. Added to this is the fact that some books simply demand more than one reading. A first reading of *Hamlet* or *Middlemarch* can do no more than scratch its surface; these are books one has to live with. For all these reasons, Nabokov famously said that "one cannot read a book; one can only reread it."[25] On the other hand, rereading takes time away from first readings. Life is short, and every time we return to an old favourite, we are deciding not to try something new—perhaps missing out on some great new discovery. For this reason, rereading is often accompanied by what Spacks calls a "guilt-inducing awareness of all the other books that you should have read at least once but haven't."[26]

Every reader has to balance these conflicting urges, and once again, there are losses no matter where the balance is struck.

For much of his column, Hornby has almost no interest in rereading. Impatient with Nabokovian platitudes, he quips that "even the snootiest critic/publisher/whatever must presumably accept that we must all, at some point, read a book for the first time. I know that the only thing brainy people do with their lives is reread great works of fiction, but surely even James Wood and Harold Bloom read before they reread?"[27] Hornby also worries that returning to the works that have mattered to him will somehow diminish them. A book that means a great deal to you is usually one that "entered your life at exactly the right time, in precisely the right place, and those conditions can never be re-created."[28] Instead of revisiting these works, we should just "leave them be."[29] Besides, Hornby writes, one of the reasons people reread old favourites is to "check whether they were really as good as we remember them being."[30] But why assume that our literary judgments become more reliable as we age? Isn't it possible that time makes our judgments *less* reliable?

When Hornby finally does have an experience of rereading, it is because of the demands of commerce. In February 2011, he is considering adapting Colm Toibin's novel *Brooklyn* for film, so he rereads it just a few months after reading it for the first time. "I haven't read a book twice in six months for decades," Hornby writes, "and the experience was illuminating."[31] He finds that his memories of the book are not altogether accurate. He did not exactly misremember or misunderstand the book; rather, he had "forgotten the proximity of narrative events in relation to each other. Some things happened sooner than I was prepared for, and others much later."[32] His admiration for the book not only stands, but is strengthened: he is newly impressed by the "precise and calm and controlled"[33] prose. Hornby's experience with rereading is positive, and it seems to dispel many of his worries about it. *Brooklyn* matters just as much to him after the second reading as it did after the first. His judgments about the book do not change radically, but seem to deepen after a fresh look. Hornby finds no reason to think that his later judgment is less reliable than his earlier one. He clearly seems to understand the novel and its merits better the second time around.

But despite this positive encounter with rereading, and despite the fact that his worries about rereading have proved groundless, Hornby doesn't do any more of it. He doesn't reread any other books—or if he does, he doesn't write about the experience. This is odd, because when Hornby makes other pleasant discoveries—of exciting new authors and genres, for example—he makes a conscious effort to incorporate them into his reading life. Having discovered young adult fiction, for example, he sets out to read more of it. But while his attitude toward rereading may change, his behavior with respect to it doesn't. Why not? Could it be that he thinks writing about rereading will not make for interesting columns? That seems unlikely: there are plenty of successful books about experiences with rereading,[34] and any reader who has followed Hornby's adventurers for five years is likely to be very interested in his encounters with books he has already read. Could it be that he has more urgent priorities—new books he is itching to read for the first time? That doesn't seem to be the case: his subsequent columns in 2011 announce no great discoveries or change in direction. More than anything, Hornby's avoidance of rereading looks like habit. He is set in his suspicion of rereading, and a first-hand encounter with how enjoyable it can be is not enough to shake him out of his rut. Inertia is also a part of Hornby's reading life.

How to Feel about Oneself as a Reader

So far, I've focused on the decisions readers make: decisions about what to read, what to reread and how to do both. But the reading life involves more than sorting out what and how to read. It is also a matter of *feeling* certain ways about one's reading, and of sorting out what these feelings are. This emotional side figures prominently in Hornby's life as a reader, and not always in ways he finds pleasant. His reflections on his reading contain a fair amount of self-criticism, even self-loathing. He chastises himself often for reading the wrong things and for reading them badly. As we have seen, in his very first column, Hornby chastises himself for not reading *Franny and Zooey* decades earlier. In his second column, he describes the sense of failure he feels for not finishing as many books as he'd like:

> Unfinished, abandoned, abandoned, unfinished. Well, you can't say I didn't warn you. In the first of these columns, I voiced the suspicion that my then-current reading jag was unsustainable; I was worried, I seem to recall, about the end of the summer, and the forthcoming football season, and it's true that both of these factors have had an adverse effect on book consumption.[35]

This sense of failure becomes a recurring feature of Stuff I've Been Reading. So do his feelings that he has read certain books badly. On finishing Tobias Wolff's *Old School*, he decides he has let the book down: "I should have read it in a sitting, but I didn't, and I never gave it a chance to leave its mark. We are never allowed to forget that some books are badly written; we should remember that sometimes they're badly read, too."[36] To be fair, Hornby doesn't think he's unique in being a bad reader. Some of the funniest passages in Stuff I've Been Reading are the ones cataloguing the sins of other, nameless readers.

(Especially funny is his description of the "laziest, most irritating book-club criticism" one can make of a novel—namely, that the reader "just didn't care" about the characters.[37]) Still, if we take Hornby at his word, his reading life is a constant battle with self-loathing and despair. He can't shake the feeling that he's letting the books down.

These feelings go hand in hand with disruptions in Stuff I've Been Reading. There are abrupt shifts in focus, attempts to take the column in new directions, and on several occasions, long periods in which Hornby stops writing it altogether. Sometimes there is no obvious trigger for his disaffection. In September 2005, and again in May 2008, he finds himself unable to concentrate on anything he reads, and wonders whether he has lost the skill of reading entire books. At other times, his interest in reading is squeezed out by other art forms. After a great concert in March 2004, for instance, Hornby spends two weeks not wanting to read at all—too "itchy" and "energized" by music to focus on books.[38] In March/April 2008, his attention captured by film, he writes a column called "Stuff I've Been Watching." But the most interesting disruptions are triggered by Hornby's domestic life. When he moves house in 2005, he is forced to reflect on his book-buying habits: just when did he think he would read all those titles from his "Books Bought" list? And shortly before his third son is born, he worries that he "will never be able to visit a bookshop again,"[39] and goes on a book-buying binge. A few weeks after the baby's arrival, Hornby worries that he is "turning into a vegetable," and immediately reads a lengthy biography of an experimental novelist—"just to prove [he] still could."[40]

Hornby's disaffection with reading peaks on the several occasions when he decides to stop writing the column. Between October 2006 and April 2007, he takes "a refreshing five-month vacation from his column."[41] Then, in September 2008, he announces he is giving it up for good. It doesn't last, of course: the column starts up again in May 2010, with Hornby comparing himself to a boomerang child who returns to his parents' house long after moving out. It would be easy to explain these breaks by pointing to factors outside the column. Maybe Hornby needs to finish a novel or a movie treatment; maybe he has too much going on in his personal life; maybe he's quarreled with the editors of the *Believer*. Whatever truth there may be in these explanations, they ignore the way that these breaks make perfect sense within the column itself. Once one has gotten used to the voice and the concerns of Stuff I've Been Reading, it doesn't seem strange at all that Hornby would take abrupt vacations from it—or even that he would vow to chuck the whole thing, only to come back a year and a half later. Hornby presents his reading life as tough, intellectually and emotionally tough—rewarding, sure, and sometimes joyous. But it's also discouraging. The books don't always hold his interest; they can't always compete with music and film; and they make him feel bad about himself. Whenever Hornby announces that the column is over, I'm no more surprised than I am when someone in a difficult marriage announces he's finally left. I'm even less surprised when he comes back.

Stories and Quests

What does Hornby's column show about the experience of reading? And what does it show about the ways in which reading is embedded in a life? The first thing to note is how varied Hornby's reading life is: how many different elements it contains, and how much tension there is among them. His decisions about what to read are governed by conflicting desires. His short-term desire to read familiar, comforting works clash with his longer-term, higher-order desire to become the sort of person who will enjoy reading different things. Furthermore, Hornby's ideas about what to read are embedded in his life in complex, tangled ways. His received ideas about what he should be reading—for instance, that he should have read *Franny and Zooey* years ago—clash with his desire to communicate the joys of reading with those who think it has to be a grim affair done out of obligation. All of these desires interact with occurrences in the rest of Hornby's life. When football season starts, he reads less; as children are born, he worries that he will stop reading altogether, and he responds by throwing himself into reading more energetically than ever. Christmas is the trigger that sends him to Dickens; rewarding encounters with music and film lead him to tinker with the column's format, even to wish he were not writing it at all. He experiments with rereading because of career pressures, but habit and inertia prevent him from repeating the experiment, despite its rewards. Above all, Hornby experiences conflicting emotions about his reading life. Moments of unselfconscious enjoyment clash with a nagging sense of duty—a sense that, despite his attempts to shout it down, never goes away. He feels constant guilt that he's not reading enough, not reading well enough, not reading the right things, not getting everything from them that he should.

The second thing to note is that despite all this diversity, Hornby's experiences as a reader are still unified. But what unifies them? Not the mere fact that they are all *his* experiences. Hornby sometimes claims to experience his reading life as lacking all unity,[42] and while this can't be literally true, it shows that his mere existence as a reader is not enough to unify his experiences in the ways that matter to him. In so far as Hornby's reading life is unified, it is unified by his column—or more accurately, by the process of reflection carried out in the column. To put it simply, Hornby's reading life is unified by his continuing effort to write a unified story about his reading life. I don't just mean that his experiences become unified because they all appear in the same magazine feature—though of course that has something to do with it. I mean something more subtle. Hornby's reflections on his reading are an attempt to discern a certain kind of story in it. Month after month, as he tries to make sense of his experiences, he brings an ideal to the process: an unstated standard that tells him what the final result ought to look like. The standard is that of a narrative with a certain kind of shape. It is a narrative that flows, with natural transitions from one episode to the next—a story in which "one book leads to another and to another."[43] It is a narrative with a direction—maybe not something definite enough to be called a *telos*, but certainly an overall shape that shows something being accomplished as time passes. It is thus a story whose overall effect demonstrates more than the sum of its individual episodes. Stuff I've Been Reading ends up being the story of how one reader tried to find a distinctive sort of intelligibility in his reading life—the intelligibility that is produced by a successful story. If this story is as much made as it is found—and it is—that does not make it sheer invention. After all, Hornby constructs his story *by living it*. His desire for a unified reading life doesn't just surface in his column at the end of the month, never to be seen again. It shapes his decisions and his actions. This month's boredom with his usual reading choices becomes next month's experiment in broadening his tastes. This month's guilt about all the titles he hasn't read becomes next month's rant against the very idea of letting duty intrude on one's reading. Actions spur further reflection, and so the cycle continues. Hornby's reading life becomes unified because he tacitly sees himself as the protagonist of a story that *ought* to be unified. If, as I have claimed, reading is a practice that pursues certain goods, then the unity of one's reading life is its overarching good. By reading, and by reflecting on one's reading, one seeks the coherence, simplicity and elegance of a good story.

These ideas may sound strange. But they're actually quite familiar. Many philosophers have noticed that our ideas about a good life tend to involve more than just the total amount of well-being contained in that life. We also want our lives to have a certain shape, to display a certain kind of narrative structure. Two lives might possess exactly the same amount of pleasure or satisfaction, but if one constitutes a more pleasing story than the other, we tend to consider it better. Michael Slote illustrates this point as follows:

> A given man may achieve political power and, once in power, do things of great value, after having been in the political wilderness throughout his earlier career. He may later die while still "in harness" and fully possessed of his powers, at a decent old age. By contrast, another man may have a meteoric success in youth, attaining the same office as the

first man and also achieving much good; but then lose power, while still young, never to regain it. Without hearing anything more, I think our natural, instinctive reaction to these examples would be that the first man was the more fortunate.[44]

If we agree that the first life is preferable to the second—and I do—it seems to be because of its narrative structure. The two lives, we are supposing, have equivalent amounts of well-being. They contain the same events, the same triumphs and disappointments. They differ only in how their events are structured. The first life is a story whose most agreeable episodes come at the end, allowing us to see the entire life as a development toward something that culminates it. The later events cast the earlier events in a new light, giving them a meaning they would not otherwise have had. The second life makes up a much less satisfying story. Its triumphs come early and perhaps too easily, leading to the disappointment of the final stages. Thought experiments such as this one seem to show that our lives possess a distinctive kind of value that might be called narrative value. We don't just care about what happens in our lives; we also care about "the story of our lives, the narrative structure of our lives."[45]

Hornby's reflections on his reading life are another example of this phenomenon, albeit in a highly specific domain. As Hornby tries to make sense of his experiences as a reader, he tries to unify these experiences by telling a coherent story about them. But not just any kind of unity will do. He tries to find in reading life a specific kind of narrative structure. He tries to view it not just as a story, but as a kind of story we find pleasing and uplifting. The genre to which Hornby is drawn is that of a *quest*: a narrative that portrays a life a search for a good that will give it meaning. A common theme of quest stories is that it is the very search for such a good, not any of the particular candidates for it, that gives a life its value. Hornby's quest demonstrates this too. Stuff I've Been Reading sets out merely to describe Hornby's search for a satisfying reading life, a reading life with unity and a distinctive shape. But what it finally shows is that the unity and the narrative structure displayed by his reading life are themselves products of this very search. Stuff I've Been Reading thus illustrates, in a specific domain, Alasdair MacIntyre's claim that "the good life for man is the life spent in seeking for the good life for man."[46]

All of this sounds unbearably precious—and in the hands of a clumsy writer, it often is. But when it works, it works spectacularly. Proust manages it fairly well. Perhaps the simplest way to characterize *In Search of Lost Time* is as the story of someone who spends a lifetime learning what he has always dimly sensed: that what makes his life a compelling story are his attempts to see it as a compelling story. Of course, most of us aren't Prousts—or Hornbys, for that matter—so most of us will never find in our lives a story as rich as *In Search of Lost Time* (or *High Fidelity*). But if we think reading can be an important part of a good life, surely part of the reason is that reflecting on our reading is a way of giving unity and shape to our lives—not just finding them there.

Of course, most readers don't have monthly columns. I suspect that most don't write about their reading lives at all. Are Hornby's experiences relevant to them? I think so. Granted, Hornby conducts his quest in an unusually explicit and self-conscious way. But the difference between his quest and that of someone who does not write about her reading life at all is one of degree rather than kind. All readers, I suspect, reflect on their activity in some ways and to some degree. That is just what it means to say that such a life consists of actions performed by agents rather than simply events that happen in a physico-causal order. To call an action, such as reading, *mine*, is to say that I recognize it as something that *I do*, and this requires the action to be, on some level, an object of my awareness. But this awareness can take many different forms, from the very explicit and self-conscious to the very unreflective and unthematized. We might imagine these forms making up a continuum stretching between two poles: perfect reflectiveness at one end, perfect unreflectiveness at the other. Both of these poles are ideals, or perhaps even fictions. The ideal of someone whose actions are entirely transparent to her seems no more realizable than the ideal of someone whose actions are utterly opaque to her. In practice, our stories are never entirely open to ourselves, and never entirely closed. We always find ourselves somewhere in the middle—in reading no less than in life.

Chapter 4

ETHICS *FROM* READING?

Improving Reading

As we've seen, one of the marks of the common reader is a sense that reading is important, even if it's hard to articulate why. This sense is often bound up with a belief that reading makes people better—not just intellectually or culturally better, but ethically better. Reading, according to this view, is a morally improving activity, one that can help develop character traits that good people need. This view is surprisingly widespread, and not just among passionate readers. A 2014 article in *Scientific American* declares that "everyone should read *Harry Potter*" because the "tales of the young wizard instill empathy."[1] The article reports that experiments conducted by psychologists at the University of Modena found that when young people read passages from the Potter novels dealing with prejudice against "Mud-bloods," they became more tolerant toward immigrants and other stigmatized groups than their peers who had not.[2] Most interesting of all, this increase in empathy didn't seem to be caused solely by the content of J. K. Rowling's novels. The study suggested that there is something about the *process* of reading that helps instill empathy and tolerance—an effect that other studies have claimed to find as well.[3] But the view that reading makes us morally better is not advanced only by psychologists. Philosophers and literary critics have defended it for decades, indeed centuries. Recent discussions of this view often cite Wayne Booth's *The Company We Keep*, an influential work of literary criticism that mounts a spirited defense of the attempt "to tie 'art' to 'life,' the 'aesthetic' to the 'practical.'"[4] Another influential statement of this view is Richard Rorty's *Contingency, Irony, and Solidarity*, which argues that certain kinds of literature can help us become aware of our capacity for cruelty and other worrisome traits.[5] Major works by Andrew Gibson,[6] Colin McGinn,[7] and many other philosophers and literature critics explore similar terrain. To be sure, not everyone thinks reading is a source of moral improvement. No less august a reader than Harold Bloom warns that "you cannot directly improve anyone's life by reading better or more deeply […] I am wary of any arguments whatsoever that connect the pleasures of solitary reading to the public good."[8] And as we saw in the last chapter, Nick Hornby is adamant that if you don't read the classics, "*nothing bad will happen to you*; more importantly, *nothing good will happen to you if you do*."[9] Still, it's significant that Bloom and Hornby find it necessary to argue so forcefully against this view. In many circles, the idea that reading makes us better is close to an orthodoxy.

Recently, however, the presuppositions of this orthodoxy have been harshly criticized. In a widely discussed op-ed piece in the *New York Times*, philosopher Gregory Currie argues that the evidence offered in support of this view is far weaker than it first appears. Yes, some studies by psychologists seem to show that reading has all sorts of morally salutary effects. But when these studies are examined closely, Currie argues, they usually turn out to document extremely narrow effects in highly artificial situations—situations that have little in common with the way people actually read. "Most of the studies," for example, "don't draw on serious literature but on short snatches of fiction devised especially for experimental purposes."[10] Worse, it's hard to imagine what good evidence in this area would even look like. "Try designing an experiment to test the effects of *War and Peace*," Currie quips. Not only does good empirical evidence not yet exist; reading is such a messy, complicated activity that it's plausible that such evidence will never exist. For this reason, Currie concludes that most of those who are convinced of the moral benefits of reading do not base their conviction on evidence at all. It is simply "a matter of faith."[11]

It's hard not to sympathize with Currie's point. Of course we shouldn't simply take for granted that reading makes people morally better. Anyone who's read or watched *A Clockwork Orange*, whose thuggish protagonist loves Beethoven as much as he does ultraviolence, will wonder just how tight the link is between aesthetic experience and moral improvement. Of course we shouldn't conclude that such a link exists before we've looked at the evidence—even though, as Currie argues, it's unclear what the relevant evidence would even look like. But at the same time, Currie's critique seems to move a tad too quickly in the other direction. Like those he criticizes, Currie seems to want to determine *whether* reading offers moral benefits without first settling the question of *how* it might do so. He wants to see whether there's a causal link between reading and becoming a better person without first sorting out which sort of causal story makes the most sense here, and is most worth investigating. We don't usually investigate causal links in that way. We don't normally ask whether a drug does or doesn't lower blood pressure without first having some idea of how or why it might do so. When we start probing the link between a putative cause and a putative effect, it's typically because we have some well-founded suspicions about why the link might be there—largely because we can tell a plausible story of how the first sort of thing might be expected to lead to the second sort of thing. So before we try to determine *whether* reading does or doesn't make us morally better, we should seek some clarity about *how* it might do so.[12] Clarification of this sort doesn't replace empirical inquiry, but it does help clear the way for it.[13]

At any rate, that's what I'd like to do in this chapter. I'd like to shed light on some of the ways in which reading might lead to moral improvement. I'll focus on several different views that philosophers have advanced about this topic, in the hope of seeing whether any of them offer a plausible explanation of why reading might make people better. My conclusions, alas, will be pessimistic. I'll argue that several of the most popular views that philosophers have advanced about this issue don't amount to a convincing case for the moral benefits of reading. Furthermore, I'll argue that one of the most serious problems with these views is that they tend to make simplistic and problematic assumptions about the nature of reading—assumptions born from a failure to look closely at the activity of reading, in itself and as such. Finally, I'll suggest that a lesser-known view defended by Paul Ricoeur shows significantly more promise than the alternatives. While I won't try to settle the debate about whether one can get an ethics from reading, I will make some suggestions about how Ricoeur's view might push the debate forward.

Finally, a caveat. Several of the theorists I'll be discussing focus on whether the reading of *literature* can be a source of moral improvement—where "literature" means, roughly, a sort of time-tested highbrow fiction exemplified by the realist novel. I won't restrict my discussion in that way. I'm interested in whether *any* sort of reading—not just the reading of a certain kind of novel—could conceivably offer moral benefits. While this is a different question than the ones asked by some of my interlocutors, it doesn't, I think, preclude them from having useful things to say about it.

The Supply-Side Approach

How have philosophers tried to explain the supposed moral benefits of reading? One popular strategy has been to focus on the nature of *what* we read: to claim that there is something *in* texts, or in certain kinds of texts, that causes us to become better people when we read them. This view might be called a "supply-side"[14] theory, since it suggests that the moral benefits of reading come from the things that are supplied to readers—not so much from what readers *do* with those features. An especially influential version of this view has been advanced by Martha Nussbaum. In her book *Poetic Justice*, Nussbaum sets out to show that "storytelling and literary imagining are not opposed to rational argument, but can provide essential ingredients in a rational argument."[15] She defends "a humanistic and multivalued conception of public rationality,"[16] one that understands moral and political judgment as an art. She claims that reading literature plays a crucial role in helping agents acquire skill at this art, and she gives two main arguments for this claim. The first is that reading literature helps us to develop an ability that she calls *fancy*. Nussbaum uses this term to refer to a certain kind of "metaphorical imagination," or the "ability to see one thing as another, to see one thing in another."[17] Fancy is the ability to see a thing as pointing beyond itself, to see "in the things that are perceptible and at hand other things that are not before one's eyes."[18] Nussbaum claims that the reading of literature strengthens this ability by teaching us that the parts of a story may have a significance that isn't immediately apparent. It shows that an episode in a narrative may symbolize something else, or reveal something crucial about a character, or play a special role in the larger narrative structure. It therefore gives us practice in looking for deeper meanings, sharpening our skills at going beyond what is immediately given. But an ability to see beyond the given is also crucial for moral and political life. "All of human life," Nussbaum argues, "is a going beyond the facts, an acceptance of generous fancies, a projection of our own sentiments and inner activities onto the forms we perceive about us."[19] In the public sphere, I observe only the actions of others. I don't perceive the thoughts and feelings that give rise to these actions. But I can interpret actions in a generous, charitable way rather than in a mean-spirited way. Moreover, I *should* interpret them generously, since agents and citizens who do so are more likely to avoid conflict and form cohesive social units than those who do not. Relating generously to others requires fancy, which Nussbaum calls a "great charity in the heart [that] nourishes a generous construal of the world."[20] She concludes that since reading develops our capacity for fancy, it is "a *cause* of better ways of living."[21]

Nussbaum's second argument concerns the effect that reading has on the emotions. Regulating the emotions is clearly an important part of moral reflection. If I'm going to judge well about moral matters, I can't be dominated by emotion. Someone who allows herself to be overwhelmed by anger or pity, for example, seems likely to judge poorly. At the same time, a good judge doesn't put her emotions entirely out of play. Someone who feels no revulsion at cruelty, or who lets this feeling play no role in her assessment of a situation, is a poor judge. Judging well about ethics and politics involves giving feelings their due while keeping them in check. As Nussbaum puts it, it involves being guided by "those, and only those, thoughts, sentiments, and fantasies that are part of a rational outlook on the world."[22] Someone who can do so is what Nussbaum calls a "judicious spectator"[23]—a term that she borrows from Adam Smith. The judicious spectator, as Smith and Nussbaum understand him, is "first of all, a spectator. That is, he is not personally involved in the events he witnesses, although he cares about the participants as a concerned friend."[24] In other words, a judicious spectator has the ability to distance himself from situations that call for moral judgment. He can control his feelings enough to view a situation with some degree of neutrality. But while the judicious spectator can view situations with some detachment, he is not "lacking in feeling."[25] On the contrary, Nussbaum claims, "among his most important moral faculties is the power of imagining vividly what it is like to be each of the persons whose situations he imagines."[26] Moral judgment is not guided by emotion alone, but neither is it devoid of emotion. It is marked by the judicious use of emotions in a process of "detached evaluation."[27] But as Nussbaum points out, the ability to evaluate in a way that is detached but not unfeeling is enhanced by reading. Reading literature teaches me to assess what I read in ways that draw on my emotions without being dominated by them. I may be moved by a character's plight, but I'm not personally affected by it. I am disinterested but not unfeeling. The more I read, and the more sensitively I read, the more practice I get using my emotions in a controlled, detached way. According to Nussbaum, it is "this sort of emotion, the emotion of the judicious spectator, that literary works construct in their readers."[28]

So for Nussbaum, reading plays two crucial roles in moral development. First, it strengthens our capacity for fancy, leaving us better able to read the actions of others in generous ways. Second, it shows us how to put the emotions in their proper place: how to judge about moral matters without falling into the traps of either cold-heartedness or sentimentality. Reading literature makes us better at moral deliberation—not because it supplements rationality with something else, but because it helps us to be rational in complex, "multivalued"[29] ways.

There's a lot here that seems right. It seems clear that reading involves looking beyond what is given, and experiencing emotions in a somewhat detached way. It also seems clear that these abilities matter for ethics and politics. Other things being equal, someone who can relate generously toward others and put emotion in its proper place probably will be a better agent and a better citizen than someone who cannot. But there is something troubling about Nussbaum's way of discussing these matters. Throughout *Poetic Justice*, she uses extremely strong language to characterize the effects that reading has on moral and political agents, speaking as though there is a direct causal link between reading literature and becoming a better person. She says, for example, that since reading improves our capacity for fancy, it is "a *cause* of better ways of living."[30] She also says that "literary works *construct* in their readers"[31] the emotions of the judicious spectator. Such language suggests that receiving ethical instruction from literature is a deterministic process, one in which texts exert certain effects on readers through a process in which readers are essentially passive. Nussbaum not only describes reading in general as functioning deterministically; she describes specific texts as quite mechanistic in their effects. She says that *Hard Times* "cultivates abilities of imagination that are essential"[32] to moral judgment, while Richard Wright's *Native Son* "constructs a reader who is a judicious and neutral judge."[33] As Simon Stow points out, Nussbaum speaks as though "there is but one valid interpretation of the text, and one lesson or set of lessons to be derived from each."[34] She also speaks as though texts neatly transmit their lessons to readers, without being mediated by interpretation. Only if we assume that texts convey their lessons in this way can we be confident that *Hard Times* and *Native Son* simply *will* make us more compassionate for victims of injustice, full stop. In short, Nussbaum tries "to discern the message that the text transmits to its audience by examining the text rather than the audience."[35] That is why her view could be called "a 'supply-side' theory of the novel"—it dismisses as irrelevant "the role of the reader in the process of deriving the relevant lessons from literature."[36]

But is the supply-side theory plausible? It might be if texts were mere objects, things that contain and dispense their meanings in the way kegs contain and dispense beer. It's certainly possible to view texts as mere containers for meaning, and to think that these meanings are what they are independently of what readers make of them. If we saw texts in this way, then it would be plausible to suggest that a given literary work has a fixed set of lessons to teach to any reader whatsoever, and to think that the work will transmit these lessons in straightforward and even deterministic ways. It would be plausible to say that *Hard Times* simply *will* cultivate our moral imagination, and that *Native Son* simply *will* turn us into more neutral judges. If, however, we have a more subtle view of what texts are and how they mean—a view that has learned from the past century's developments in hermeneutics and literary theory—then we will likely be far more skeptical of Nussbaum's view. This is a big topic, and I can only touch on it here. Suffice it to say that many of us agree with Hans-Georg Gadamer when he says that what we naively call *the* text is "not an object at all [but] a *relationship*"[37]—an interaction between readers and the forces of tradition. As Gadamer sees it, what I identify as *the* text is not a mere object at all, but is to some degree a product of my biases and interpretive activity. At the same time, these biases and interpretive acts are not self-contained. They have themselves been shaped by forces of culture and tradition, including the very forces they seek to interpret. On this view, the reading of a literary work is not an adequation of a subject and an object, but rather "a historically effected event"[38] involving a fusion of two horizons that cannot be understood apart from each other. If we view texts and interpretation as Gadamer does, then we will be reluctant to think of the lessons of literature as simply transmitted from self-contained texts to passive readers. We'll see these lessons as shaped by readers through interpretation, and we'll probably conclude, with Gadamer, that "the very idea of a definitive interpretation [is] intrinsically contradictory."[39] In short, to those of us drawn to a Gadamerian view of texts and meaning, the supply-side theory just does not look plausible. We must find a different account of reading, one that grants that what literary works teach us depends on who reads them, and how, and why.

The Conversational Approach

But how, exactly, could the moral lessons of reading depend on readers? To answer this question, I'd like to turn to another account of reading that has been offered by Simon Stow. As we've seen, Stow harshly criticizes the supply-side approach. He criticizes Nussbaum in particular for what he sees as her naiveté about interpretation. He proposes instead that if we wish to explain how reading can be ethically valuable, we should focus not just on the contents of literary works, but on the process of responding to such works. He notes that one of the ways we respond to literary works is by talking about them. When a book moves us, either positively or negatively, we want to discuss it with others. Jay Parini puts it this way: "When I read something, I want to talk about it. I want to compare it with other texts. I want to match my own voice with the voice of the text. That is what it means to be a thinking person."[40] The existence of reading groups is a testament to literature's ability to get us talking. Stow builds on this point to claim that "there is something beneficial about the *process* of discussion"[41] that transcends the particular works being discussed. Specifically, the process of discussing literature trains us to discuss controversial and charged issues productively. As Nussbaum observes, judging well about moral matters requires that we not be dominated by emotion. Stow points out that a similar ability matters for social and political life. In a healthy community, citizens need to discuss matters of common concern in a civil way. They need to discuss sensitive issues without being dominated by their emotions or their interests. Reading might make a useful contribution here, since it often provokes conversations that provide "an opportunity for citizens to talk about their fears, concerns and desires."[42] When citizens raise their concerns and desires while discussing literature, they do so "at a level of abstraction that arises from being seen to talk about literary events and literary characters rather than directly about themselves."[43] This detachment makes it easier for them to discuss sensitive topics. They "talk about issues that they would not normally bring to a public forum; and […] talk about them in a way that allows for a more considered approach to such matters than might emerge if they were seen to be talking about their own concerns."[44] Such conversations inevitably tend to be self-centered. "When we talk about literature," Stow claims, "we are, in a way, talking about *ourselves*."[45] This is another lesson taught by reading groups. In talking about a book, the issues we most want to discuss are typically not the ones that a neutral judge would deem most central to it. Instead, they're the ones that matter most to us, the ones we were most inclined to discuss before we started reading. Talking about reading is narcissistic, and according to Stow, "rather than trying to find some methodology which will emancipate us from this perspective, [we should] *embrace* it."[46] The moral and political benefits of reading result not from literary works themselves, but from their ability to get us talking about our own concerns. What matters is the fact that we are talking—not the works we are supposedly talking *about*.

Clearly, Stow's position avoids the worst dangers of the supply-side theory. It avoids the naiveté involved in saying that literary works construct justice and sensitivity in readers without any contribution from those readers. Stow grants that what we see in a text depends on what we bring to it. More importantly, he argues that we can recognize this dependence and still see reading as morally and politically valuable. For Stow, the ethical value of a literary work doesn't depend on its containing a fixed slate of lessons that are mechanistically transmitted to readers. Instead, it depends on what readers *do* as a result of their encounter with the text. Stow also leaves open the possibility that different readers will respond to this encounter in very different ways. What *Hard Times* says to me may be very different from what it says to you. For all these reasons, Stow's position has considerable appeal.

But it also faces problems of its own. For Stow, literary works matter for ethics because they're catalysts. Their value lies in their ability to get us talking about our concerns and fears. This ability is, we might say, formal, in that it doesn't depend on anything intrinsic to particular literary works. This view has some surprising consequences. First, it suggests that any work whatsoever might prove ethically valuable, at least under the right circumstances. If a work's value for ethics lies not in its content but in the fact that people want to discuss is, then any work that people want to discuss will, by virtue of that fact, be ethically valuable. Dickens and Wright might have no more intrinsic ethical significance than the latest airport potboilers. If a given audience finds the potboilers more stimulating of conversation, then the potboilers will have more ethical value for the audience in question. Similarly, no one of Dickens's works will be intrinsically more valuable for ethics than any other. *The Pickwick Papers* will have just as much ethical significance as *Hard Times*—more, if people happen to prefer talking about it. Finally, since talking is what matters, reading will be no more valuable for ethics than any other activity that makes people talk. Watching sports and drinking wine might prove just as valuable as reading Dickens, if not more so.

All of this seems wrong. It just seems to be a fact that some literary works, and some practices, are more ethically significant than others. This greater significance must have something to do with their content—with, for example, something intrinsic to *Hard Times* that makes it more ethically significant than *The Pickwick Papers*, airport potboilers or wine drinking. No doubt it will be difficult to spell out what "intrinsic" can possibly mean here; no doubt our access to a work's "intrinsic" character must be mediated by interpretation. But if reading matters for ethics, the explanation must have something to do with the works read. These works can't be mere catalysts. Their value can't lie simply in the way they provoke activities that have no necessary connection with them and that might be triggered in indefinitely many other ways.

A compromise position is needed. We need to recognize that the ethical value of reading is tied to specific works, while granting that readers play a role in interpreting these lessons. We need to see literary works as having specific ethical content, without claiming that this content instructs readers in deterministic ways. Let me now explain why I think Paul Ricoeur's account of reading can help us articulate such a position.

A Hermeneutical Approach

Ricoeur's most sustained discussion of reading appears in Volume Three of *Time and Narrative*. Throughout this book, Ricoeur distances himself from what he sees as the reckless conclusions drawn by some adherents of poststructuralism and deconstruction. He is especially troubled by the Derridean suggestion that there is nothing outside the text, and he insists that a defining feature of narratives is the way they interact with an extra-textual reality. Ricoeur writes:

> I fight against the claim that texts constitute by themselves a world or a closed world [...] It is only in libraries that texts are closed on themselves—and even then only when nobody reads them. So then, we have a closed world of texts in a library, but literature is not a big library. It is by the act of reading that I follow a certain trajectory, a trajectory of meaning of the text. Then I reenact in a certain sense the dynamic course of the text and I prolong this dynamic beyond the text itself.[47]

In short, narratives refer to reality. That said, they don't just point out aspects of reality that exist independently of them. They interact with reality in a more subtle way. Ricoeur claims that narratives open onto reality thanks to the mediation of reading. Reading establishes a link "between the fictive world of the text and the actual world of the reader. The effects of fiction, effects of revelation and transformation, are essentially effects of reading."[48] "Revelation" and "transformation" are crucial terms here. The most noticeable effect that narratives have on reality is to change those who read them; and they change readers by showing readers something, revealing something that may have gone unnoticed before the text was read. It isn't surprising that Ricoeur says this, given his debts to Gadamer. Gadamer famously argues that genuine understanding occurs only in application.[49] On this view, I don't fully understand a text until I can apply it to concrete cases, and in particular, until I can explain what it has to say to my own existential situation. Ricoeur's claims about reading echo Gadamer's view, and suggest that understanding a narrative is a matter of letting it transform me.

But how should this transformation be described? Ricoeur resists the temptations to which Nussbaum and Stow succumb. He doesn't say that being transformed by a text involves passively receiving certain lessons from it, lessons that remain constant from reader to reader. Nor does he say that being transformed is a matter of performing activities (such as talking) that have no intrinsic link with what one reads. He opts for a very different vocabulary, claiming that when texts are read, they open up *worlds* for their readers. The term "world" comes with a great deal of baggage, since it is a key term for the phenomenological tradition from which Ricoeur emerges. For both Husserl and Heidegger, the term "world" refers not to a collection of things, not to the totality of objects, but to the contexts in which subjects encounter objects as meaningful. The later Husserl famously speaks of the "life world" that is presupposed by all our dealings with objects but that can never be fully objectified. Similarly, the early Heidegger understands a world—which he calls "that *'wherein'* a factical Dasein as such can be said to 'live'"[50]—as the set of meaning relations that link one to other entities. When Ricoeur says that narratives open up worlds for their readers, he clearly means to invoke the full range of connotations that this term has in phenomenological philosophy.[51] At a minimum, he wants to suggest that narratives put readers in new contexts, potentially changing their ways of relating to other things.

But how? What sort of change does Ricoeur have in mind here? In a revealing passage from his essay "The Model of the Text," Ricoeur describes a world as

> the ensemble of references opened up by the text. Thus we speak about the "world" of Greece, not to designate any more what were the situations for those who lived them, but to designate the non-situational references that [...] are offered as possible modes of being, as symbolic dimensions of our being-in-the-world. For me, this is the referent of all

literature: no longer the *Umwelt* of the ostensive references of dialogue, but the *Welt* projected by the nonostensive references of every text that we have read, understood, and loved.[52]

"Possible modes of being" is the key phrase here. When I read a literary work, it presents me with ways in which I might exist, or as Ricoeur puts it, "a *proposed world* that I could inhabit and wherein I could project one of my ownmost possibilities."[53] I respond to this revelation by exploring how I might enact the existential possibilities delineated by the work. Consider what happens when I read *Hamlet*. The text presents me with a dramatization of possible ways of existing—notably, possible ways of relating to death. I see the prince grapple with the reality and the horror of death. I watch as Hamlet is first paralyzed by this insight, but ultimately learns to accept it and act in the face of it. If, like Gadamer and Ricoeur, we think that understanding a text involves letting it speak to something in me, then we will suspect that understanding *Hamlet* is a matter of asking how the prince's insights into death could be incorporated into my own existence. To understand the play is to imagine what it would be like to relate to my own death as Hamlet does, and to ask whether and in what ways I ought to do so. In Ricoeur's words, to understand a literary work is "not to project oneself into the text but to expose oneself to it; it is to receive a self enlarged by the appropriation of the proposed worlds that interpretation unfolds."[54]

The crucial point here is that this enlarging of the self is an ethical matter. As I read, I encounter new modes of being, new possibilities for my own existence. I ask which ones I ought to appropriate. Reading a text, having it disclose a world for me, is an exercise in asking which of its modes of being I ought to adopt, how I should act. The reading life is therefore a life spent immersing oneself in possible answers to the question of how one ought to live. No doubt it's possible to do so in better and worse ways; no doubt some readers are more reflective, more sensitive and more responsible explorers than others. But for all readers, literary works are an important source of raw materials for the ethical life. Ricoeur therefore says that "the thought experiments we conduct in the great laboratory of the imaginary are also explorations in the realm of good and evil."[55]

What does all this have to do with Nussbaum and Stow? Ricoeur's account of reading is valuable because it avoids the pitfalls in both of their accounts. The worlds disclosed by reading, as Ricoeur describes them, have two crucial features. First, they are disclosed *by particular readers*, through particular acts of interpretation and projection. A world is an imaginative variation on some reader's existence—or as Gerald Bruns puts it, a reader's existence viewed in a magical looking glass.[56] Narratives help me explore the realm of good and evil only when I apply them to my situation. Each reader will receive unique instruction from a given work, since learning from the work just is a matter of seeing how it might change one's own existence. So Ricoeur is no supply-sider. A work's ethical significance is not just a result of its content. A text offers no instruction at all until it interacts with some specific reader. Second, Ricoeur also denies that works are mere catalysts that lead us to perform some free-floating activity. Receiving ethical instruction from literature involves seeing how the particular existential possibilities described by a text could be incorporated into my existence. *Hamlet*, *Hard Times* and *Native Son* all have quite specific things to say to me. I can't derive just any lessons I like from them. Granted, the worlds they disclose to me are always *my* worlds, formed through my interpretive acts. But they arise from my interaction with possibilities delineated *by the text*.

The reason Ricoeur is confident in this last claim has to do with his larger theory of narrative. To summarize dramatically, Ricoeur argues that all narratives, whether fictional or historical, manifest three related structuring activities: prefiguration, configuration and refiguration, or as he playfully calls them, mimesis$_1$, mimesis$_2$ and mimesis$_3$.[57] Every narrative is an imitation of action: it describes what certain characters do over a specific stretch of time. It therefore connects events by organizing them into intelligible wholes. But according to Ricoeur, three types of structure, and three types of intelligibility, are at work here. The first, mimesis$_1$, is a kind of structuring that is implicit in all actions as such. Even before we describe actions linguistically, they have features that allow them to be described and understood. They are structured by their subordination of means to ends, for example, and by the way their parts unfold in time. Events lend themselves to being narrated because they are *prefigured* in these ways. The second type of mimesis, mimesis$_2$, refers to the intelligible structure events acquire when they become part of a written or spoken story. A story takes individual episodes and *configures* them into an intelligible whole. These episodes become part of a plot, and they derive significance from the role they play in this larger structure. Mimesis$_3$, or *refiguration*, is what Gadamer would call application. It involves the intelligibility that stories get from being explicitly read and interpreted. Stories are fully understood only when they are appropriated by some reader. Mimesis$_3$ is Ricoeur's name for this process of making sense of a story in light of who one is and where one is. Each type of mimesis, each type of intelligibility, has a structure that mirrors that of the other two. When I describe actions in a written story, I organize them in a way that parallels the organization they already have simply because they are actions. I also bestow intelligibility on them in a way that parallels the way readers make sense of the stories they read.

The crucial point is that for Ricoeur, reading—the explicit appropriation of narratives that occurs in mimesis$_3$—is a *re*-figuring of structures that narratives already possess. Narratives already possess these structures as a result of the configurational activity that Ricoeur calls mimesis$_2$. But the configuration found in mimesis$_2$ is in turn constrained by the ordering implicit in events themselves owing to prefiguration, or mimesis$_1$. To learn from a text is to re-figure its structures in a new context. Each reader performs this activity for herself, in her own way. But it is a re-figuring of structures that the text already possesses. When I ask what a literary work can tell me about how to live, I am not merely inventing. Nor am I simply reading something off the text. I am interpreting certain lessons, but lessons found *in the text*. I am playing a creative role, but my creativity is constrained by something independent of me.

Where This Leaves Us

Now let's return to the issue with which this chapter began. In response to Currie, I claimed that we shouldn't try to determine whether reading makes us morally better until we've gained some clarity on how it might do so. If my discussion of Nussbaum, Stow and Ricoeur is on the right track, we're now in a position to say something more substantive about this matter. As we've seen, the proposals made by Nussbaum and Stow don't look terribly promising. There's little reason to think that the content of a text, on its own, could cause readers to acquire morally beneficial traits. Likewise, there's little reason to think that the activity of talking about what we read, on its own, could lead directly to morally beneficial effects. But notice that both of these proposals focus on actualities. For both Nussbaum and Stow, the question of whether reading offers moral benefits boils down to the question of whether it brings something into existence—either character traits that readers actually possess, or a process of discussion that readers actually carry out. So it's not surprising that Currie's criticisms are so damaging to these approaches. If the moral benefits of reading hinge on its actually leading to particular effects, then questions about empirical evidence or the lack of it are decisive. If we can't find empirical evidence that reading actually does have the effects in question, then there's nothing more to say about the issue.

Ricoeur suggests another way of thinking about the matter. He doesn't claim that reading will give rise to actual character traits or actual processes of discussion at all. He claims that reading can open up certain *possibilities*, certain potential ways of existing that might or might not be actualized. This is a much more modest claim, because the possibilities in question aren't opened up in a foolproof or mechanistic way. They won't be opened up at all unless fairly stringent conditions are met. Being exposed to a work's content isn't enough; the reader has to *do* something in response to it. At the same time, doing something—talking about a book with others, for example—isn't enough either, since readers must attend scrupulously to the specific possibilities disclosed by specific texts. It seems plausible to suggest that much of the time, these conditions won't be met, and reading won't actually have the moral effects it could have. So if we view reading as Ricoeur does, we may have to abandon the claim that reading simply makes us better—full stop. The most we can say is that reading gives us new moral possibilities. It makes certain kinds of improvement possible.

This might seem like a laughably weak conclusion. Who cares about merely possible improvement—especially when so many of those who philosophize about reading promise *actual* improvement? What's more, possibilities can be actualized for ill as well as for good. A well-read reader might have certain admirable possibilities opened up to her—Alyosha's kindness, for instance—but also less admirable ones, such as Ivan's haughtiness or Smerdyakov's sociopathy. Who's to say that encountering new ways of being won't have morally harmful effects rather than beneficial ones? It's hard not to be sympathetic to criticisms of this sort. There's obviously a big difference between being good and being *able* to be good. But it doesn't follow that the disclosing of possibilities effected by reading is morally neutral, or worse. On the contrary, in the right circumstances, the development of certain possibilities for action is itself a moral achievement. Becoming able to do more things can itself be a form of moral improvement—even if it's possible to exercise this ability in neutral or vicious ways. This is one of the insights of the capabilities approach to well-being developed by Amartya Sen and (interestingly enough) Martha Nussbaum—though Sen and Nussbaum see the capabilities approach as a position in political theory rather than moral theory.[58] The idea behind the capabilities approach is that if we want to determine the level of development in a society, it's not enough to look at measures such as economic growth, because rapid economic growth is compatible with large numbers of people in that society living wretched lives. We must instead focus on the concrete capabilities possessed in that society—that is, on what people in that society are actually able to do. They should, for example, be able "to have good health," "to be secure against violent assault," and "to imagine, think, and reason […] in a 'truly human' way."[59] There's no guarantee that those with lots of possibilities open to them will use them for good rather than ill. Someone with access to good food might eat unhealthily; someone with ample leisure time might waste it. The point is simply that the presence of certain capabilities is a precondition for a society's being healthy. There's much more to a good life than having capabilities, but in the absence of certain capabilities, it's impossible for a life to be good.

I think an analogous claim can be made about morality. The question of what sorts of things an agent is capable of doing is relevant to the moral status of that agent's life. Having a certain range of possibilities is a precondition of living a good life. Part of being able to lead a flourishing life is having a certain range of existential possibilities. And the main reason that reading is morally interesting is that it can enhance one's range of existential possibilities. By disclosing new worlds, it helps provide readers with the raw materials for a good life, broadening and deepening the existential options available to them. As with the capabilities discussed by Sen and Nussbaum, having these possibilities disclosed to one doesn't guarantee that one will make good use of them. Some readers might fail to actualize any of the possibilities opened up through what they read. And others—perhaps impressed by *American Psycho* or *Mein Kampf*—might actualize horrifying ones. The point is simply that unless a significant range of possibilities is available, it's hard to imagine a life being good at all. In short, reading shouldn't be seen as a cause of better ways of living, but that doesn't make it morally neutral or worse. Its significance for morality lies in its ability to put in place the *conditions* of better ways of living.

A further advantage of Ricoeur's approach to this issue concerns the *way* reading does this. Any piece of moral theory that gives a central role to possibilities and capabilities runs the risk of being abstract and empty. After all, it's quite natural to view capabilities as mere undifferentiated potential—as a capacity that could be directed in indefinitely many directions. When viewed in this way, they're bound to appear uninteresting, as well as problematic. Possibilities and capabilities are interesting only when they're determinate: when they're seen as the concrete power to do something in particular. The worlds opened up by reading are determinate in this way, because they're essentially variations on my life as I've lived it up to now. Ricoeur calls them "imaginative variations" on the reader's current existence. They're not the undifferentiated potential to do anything at all; they're a tweaking of a particular life, a concrete variation on my life as it currently is. What's more, it's a concrete variation provoked by an equally concrete text. To respond to *Hamlet*, for example, isn't just to see that my life could be different than it is right now. It is to see that my life could be different in the specific ways proposed by the text.

What all this suggests is that the question of how reading improves us, when it does, doesn't have a general answer. Reading's moral effects vary as much as the possibilities reading opens up—which is to say that they vary as much as the things we read and the lives of readers. So rather than asking whether it does or doesn't make readers better, we should instead ask what effects the reading of *this* text might have on *that* reader in *these* concrete circumstances. The moral consequences of reading come into view only when reading is seen as a thing of this world.

Chapter 5

ETHICS *OF* READING?

Responsible Readers

In the last chapter, I explored the idea that there could be an ethics derived *from* reading. In this chapter, I'll turn to a related question: is there such a thing as an ethics *of* reading?[1] Is the act of reading itself governed by moral norms?[2] Lots of common readers think it is. A recurring theme in their reflections on reading is the idea that we mustn't read in just any way we like. There are, we're told, right and wrong ways to read, and we have a moral obligation to engage in the right ones and avoid the wrong. The norms that supposedly govern reading are different from the hypothetical norms that apply whenever we try to achieve some personal goal. When I read a textbook, I might want to remember what I read, and if I have this goal, then it makes sense for me not to read too quickly. But the responsibilities that many common readers claim to have are different: less instrumental, more impersonal and more like the duties we owe to other people. I may get everything I want out of a book; I may get all the amusement or edification I was looking for when I picked it up. But plenty of common readers would say that my duties as a reader go beyond these personal wants and needs. I owe something to what I read, and if I fail to deliver, I am doing something wrong.

It's easy to find examples of this attitude. In *How to Read a Book*, Mortimer Adler describes reading as a conversation in which the reader has a duty to "hold up his end."[3] According to Adler, the reader has a responsibility to engage critically, but not rashly, with what he reads. He must not disagree right away, but even more important, he must not agree right away. As Adler sees it, this approach to reading is more than just an effective way for readers to achieve their goals. A good book "*deserves* a good reading," and "the undemanding reader fails to satisfy this requirement."[4] More recently, Alan Jacobs has criticized Adler's "self-help, self-improvement model of reading," lamenting that much of the reading public "can't take its readerly pleasure straight but has to cut it with a sizable chunk of duty."[5] But Jacobs doesn't hesitate to say that readers have other, different responsibilities. He argues that the "one dominant, overarching, nearly definitive principle for reading" is that we should "read at whim"[6]—read whatever brings us genuine pleasure and joy. Jacobs adds that this criterion "sounds more simple and straightforward than it is,"[7] since we don't always know what our whims are. They must be cultivated and discerned by that part of our nature "that knows itself and therefore seeks *what is really good*."[8] But while Jacobs disagrees with Adler about which responsibilities readers have, he's every bit as sure that they have them.

The idea that readers have responsibilities is so widespread that we might not notice how strange it is. But it is strange, and it raises questions that aren't at all easy to answer. First, to what, or whom, do readers have these responsibilities? With many ethical claims, it's fairly clear who the recipient of our duties is supposed to be: another person, or a future generation, or myself, for example. But who or what is on the receiving end of my duty to read in a certain way? It's not clear. Second, what is the basis of the responsibilities of readers? In virtue of what do readers have them, and why do they have these precise responsibilities rather than others? In some areas of ethics, questions like these are relatively easy to answer. When asked why it's wrong to lie, for example, a Kantian can reply that doing so treats other persons as mere means, not as ends in themselves, and therefore fails to acknowledge the unconditional value all rational beings have. But in virtue of what could I be obliged to read in one way rather than another? It's not clear. So while it's natural to think that readers have responsibilities, it's not at all clear how to make sense of these responsibilities.

My goal in this chapter is to make some suggestions about how to think about these matters. I want to ask what sense we can make of the idea that readers have responsibilities, as well as ask what basis those responsibilities could possibly have. Specifically, I want to describe and assess three general strategies for understanding the responsibilities of readers. I call these strategies the *deontological*, the *alterior* and the *eudaimonistic*. I'll argue that all three strategies face serious problems, but that the third is more promising than the other two. Even the third strategy, however, needs to be modified in ways that might seem counterintuitive, and at the end of the chapter, I'll make some suggestions about how to do so. Briefly, I'll argue that the idea that there is an ethics of reading is more plausible when we view reading as a practice, in Alasdair MacIntyre's sense: a "cooperative human activity through which goods internal to that form of activity are realized."[9] If I'm right about this, reading will turn out to be a less individualistic pursuit than it first seems: not just a private diversion, and certainly not an instrument that individuals can use in any way they like. Reading will look more like a manifestation of a tradition, a communal enterprise that is extended through history and governed by norms that reflect this history. In short, I'll argue that if we want to understand the responsibilities of readers, we should pay close attention to reading's social and historical dimensions.

In what follows, I won't try to prove that readers actually do have moral responsibilities. For the sake of argument, I'll simply assume that they do, and ask what those responsibilities could possibly be like. This assumption is obviously controversial. But it's so widespread in discussions of reading that, for my purposes, it seems a safe one to make. I also won't try to answer the most interesting question about the responsibilities of readers: precisely which responsibilities do readers have? I'll table this question because the questions that I will raise—to what are readers responsible, and why—seem much more fundamental. We have to ask what the responsibilities of readers are like before trying to determine exactly what those responsibilities are.

Two Kinds of Responsibilities

Let me start by anticipating an objection. We might think that there's nothing mysterious about the responsibilities of readers, since reading is simply an instrument that individuals use to achieve their goals. All activities have goals, and if we want to achieve these goals, we have to perform the activities in certain ways rather than others. If I don't go to the driving range, I won't become a good golfer. If being a good golfer is my goal, then I ought to go to the driving range. This "ought" is purely hypothetical. The driving range is a means that helps me achieve an end I happen to have. I need not have that end, and if I didn't, my responsibility to go to the driving range would vanish. It's tempting to think that the responsibility to read in one way rather than another is exactly like this: something that binds us because it helps us achieve ends we happen to have. On this view, if I ought to read what amuses me, that can only be because I have the goal of being amused. I might not have that goal, and if I didn't, the "ought" would lose all force. Similarly, on this view, if I have a responsibility to engage critically with the books I read, that can only be because doing so helps me get what I want out of a book—information, edification and so on. If I didn't want these things, my duty to read critically would disappear. In short, it's tempting to think that the norms that govern reading are hypothetical, and that looking for a deeper basis for them is pointless.

No doubt some of the responsibilities readers think they have are actually hypothetical imperatives bound up with optional goals. Several of Adler's rules for reading seem to fall into this category: when he tells us to read actively and to ask questions as we go, these are clearly strategies for extracting information from what we read, and thus for achieving our private purposes. But not all the responsibilities attributed to readers can be explained in this way. Many of them look more categorical than hypothetical: norms that we must follow regardless of our intentions, norms that bind us *just because*. I've already mentioned some examples from Adler's *How to Read a Book*, such as his claim that good books "deserve" good readings. A more striking example appears in Virginia Woolf's essay "How Should One Read a Book?" In this essay, Woolf gives some very detailed instructions about how to read. First, she warns us to put our prejudices out of play and be entirely open to what we read. "Do not," she says,

> dictate to your author; try to become him. Be his fellow-worker and accomplice [...] [I]f you open your mind as widely as possible, then signs and hints of almost imperceptible fineness, from the twist and turn of the first sentences, will bring you into the presence of a human being unlike any other. Steep yourself in this, acquaint yourself with this, and soon you will find that your author is giving you, or attempting to give you, something far more definite.[10]

After the steeping, we must "pass judgment" on what we have read—"but not directly. Wait for the dust of reading to settle [...] Then suddenly without our willing it, for it is thus that Nature undertakes these transitions, the book will return, but differently."[11] Judging well is a demanding process. It requires that we read "slowly and unprofessionally," and judge "with great sympathy and yet with great severity."[12] It also demands that we actively compare books; that we "read widely enough and with enough understanding to make such comparisons alive and illuminating";[13] and that we share our responses with others, so that "the judgments we pass steal into the air and become part of the atmosphere which writers breathe."[14] Woolf doesn't present these rules as instruments for achieving goals readers happen to have. On the contrary, their whole effect is to transform the reader and her goals, replacing the reader as she is with something richer. Woolf speaks not of using authors for our own purposes, but of "becoming" the author. She calls the author's presence "the presence of a human being unlike any other," a presence in which we must "steep" ourselves. She speaks—colourfully, but still earnestly—of Nature directing the process through which our view of a book changes. None of this is language we would use to describe a mere instrument. For Woolf, the norms that govern reading are not mere tools at the disposal of the self. They are a way of replacing the self and its goals with something larger.

So how should we make sense of these norms? Perhaps the best way to start is to build on insights from other areas. We know, or think we know, how to defend ethical claims about topics other than reading. When we reflect on our responsibilities to other people or to non-human animals, we have a good idea to what or whom we are responsible. We also think we know why we have these responsibilities. If we can determine why we think we know these things, we might be able to apply the relevant insights to reading. Let's consider some common strategies for making sense of ethical claims.

A Deontological Approach

The first is what I'll call a *deontological* approach. In general terms, a deontological approach to ethics is based on the idea that "certain acts must or must not be done, regardless to some extent of the consequences […] [C]ertain acts are right or wrong in themselves."[15] According to views of this sort, the rightness or wrongness of an action isn't just a function of, say, the amount of pleasure or pain it brings into the world. Certain actions are obligatory or prohibited, *just because*. Crucial to a deontological approach is the idea that in some spheres, we find ourselves in the presence of a special sort of thing that's entitled to a special sort of consideration. Human rights are an obvious example: they're alleged to be entitlements or protections we have not because they are expedient, but simply because we're human beings. Kant's categorical imperative is another example. According to Kant, the reason I must treat rational beings as ends in themselves is that, as rational beings, they have unconditional value. I might find it useful to trample your rights or treat you as a mere means. But doing so would be wrong, since it would fail to treat human beings in the way they deserve to be treated.

A deontological view of readers' responsibilities might say that when we read, we are in the presence of something with a special sort of value that makes a special sort of claim on us. This isn't a result of the thing's usefulness. A book might demand a certain critical response simply because it deserves it, to use Adler's language. This sounds strange, but there are ways of cashing it out that make it less strange—or at least, no more strange than the claim that all rational beings are ends in themselves with absolute value. Moreover, the deontological view fits well with the unconditional character that claims about the responsibilities of readers often have. Consider this story told by Anne Fadiman:

> When I was eleven and my brother was thirteen, our parents took us to Europe. At the Hotel d'Angleterre in Copenhagen, as he had done virtually every night of his literate life, Kim left a book facedown on the bedside table. The next afternoon, he returned to find the book closed, a piece of paper inserted to mark the page, and the following note, signed by the chambermaid, resting on its cover:

SIR, YOU MUST NEVER DO THAT TO A BOOK.

My brother was stunned. How could it have come to pass that he—a reader so devoted that he'd sneaked a book and a flashlight under the covers at his boarding school every night after lights out—had been branded as *someone who didn't love books*?[16]

The chambermaid's reaction doesn't suggest that placing a book facedown has unfortunate consequences, making the book less valuable or harder to use. It suggests that the book has been violated—that it's simply wrong to treat a book in this way, regardless of the consequences. It's easy to dismiss reactions of this sort as hyperbolic or confused. But they appear so often in discussions of reading that they must be taken seriously. A deontological approach to reading does so.

The challenge faced by a deontological approach is to explain what readers are responsible *to*. What is the readerly equivalent of Kant's rational beings with unconditional value? If we take Fadiman's story seriously, we might say that it's the *book* to which her brother is responsible. But by "book," we can't just mean a physical object, since the point of her story is that we have responsibilities toward books that we don't have toward other medium-sized dry goods. We must instead mean the book's contents, the text as opposed to its physical tokens: not this copy of *Middlemarch*, but whatever is common to all copies of *Middlemarch*, electronic as well as paper. There is some precedent for such a view. Literary theorist Georges Poulet says that when I read, "what I hold in my hands is no longer just an object, or even simply a living thing," but "a consciousness."[17] But even if we grant Poulet's claim, it's hard to see how a text could be the kind of thing that, simply because it *is* that kind of thing, makes unconditional claims on us. As Martha Nussbaum points out, one of the more attractive things about reading is that "I can treat a book as I would never think it right to treat a real live person."[18] I might turn to books when I want "complete numbing distraction,"[19] whereas someone else in search of distraction might hire a prostitute. Hiring a prostitute seems ethically problematic, since it involves using another person for private gratification in a way that is at least potentially debasing. There doesn't seem to be any similar problem with using a book for stress relief. Books don't seem to be the sort of thing we can debase in the way we would a person.

Could it be *authors* to whom readers have responsibilities? That sounds plausible, since authors are human beings and thus deserving of all sorts of consideration we do not owe to mere things. Perhaps it's wrong to mistreat a book because doing so manifests a lack of respect for the author and her value as a conscious being. But again, it's surprisingly hard to pin down what we mean by the author here. We can't mean what literary theorists call the flesh-and-blood author, the human being who actually penned a particular work. To say this would court the intentional fallacy: that is, the mistake of understanding literary works in terms of their authors' purposes. Reading a book places me in no particular relation to its flesh-and-blood author; reading *Middlemarch* gives me no particular access to George Elliot's consciousness—or even her gender. The author to whom I relate through reading can only be what Wayne Booth calls the *implied author*: an "implied image of the artist" that readers construct on the basis of what they read.[20] Because the implied author is a construction, it is not a person, but rather an extension of the text. If, however, texts are not the sort of things to which we have unconditional responsibilities, then it's hard to see how artifacts built solely on the basis of texts could be.

The lesson seems to be that the deontological approach faces insuperable difficulties in pinning down what readers are responsible *to*. Neither of the two obvious candidates—the book or the author—is the right sort of thing.

An Alterior Approach

The next strategy I will consider could be called the *alterior*. I use this term as an adjective formed from the noun "alterity," meaning "otherness."[21] I use this term to name a way of thinking about ethics that says our main responsibility—perhaps, ultimately, our only responsibility—is to respect the otherness of others, rather than reducing it to a mode of my being. This view is most closely associated with Emmanuel Levinas, who defines ethics as a "calling into question of my spontaneity by the presence of the Other" (*Autrui*). To Levinas, ethics originates in a direct encounter with an other that is absolutely different from me and that issues me a command: "you shall not commit murder."[22] By "murder," Levinas means not just actual murder, but any attempt to abolish the other's uniqueness. I do this whenever I demand that others conform to my ideas or expectations, or whenever I think there is nothing more to a particular being than is expressed by the general categories under which I subsume it. Levinas believes that the kind of thinking done by philosophers and scientists always risks doing this. "Theory," for Levinas, "designates comprehension—the logos of being—that is, a way of approaching the known being such that its alterity with regard to the knowing being vanishes."[23] Whatever one makes of these claims, they are a natural fit with the topic of reading. One of the main goals readers have is to encounter new and different things: have vicarious experiences, learn new facts, inhabit someone else's perspective on the world. Wolfgang Iser goes so far as to describe reading as a process of "thinking the thoughts of another."[24] Moreover, good readers are often described as ones who respect the uniqueness of the things they read: ones who read texts "in their own terms" rather than distorting them with their biases and preoccupations. Colin Davis has turned this insight into a full-blown theory of reading, arguing that

> in reading, as in all encounters with other people or other cultures, what is at stake is our ability to experience an occurrence which is not defined in advance, to accept the risk and challenge of an event that does not correspond to any expectations that we might have of it.[25]

Davis uses the term "*altericide*, the murder of the Other,"[26] to describe the violence involved in trying to reduce the other to a mode of my own being. Building on his claim, we might say that the responsibilities of readers are responsibilities to the alterity of what they read—not the author, and not the text, but some sort of irreducible uniqueness glimpsed through the text. And we might say, with Davis, that this responsibility has the same source as the command "you shall not commit murder." It is an immediate, non-negotiable duty stemming from the nature of otherness itself.

In assessing this approach, the first thing to note is that it seems to face the same difficulty as the deontological approach. Like the author, the otherness I glimpse while reading isn't something I encounter directly. It's something mediated by the text, perhaps even a postulate constructed out of the text. But if texts aren't the sort of thing to which I can have unconditional responsibilities, then it's hard to see how an artifact constructed out of the text could be such a thing. Furthermore, even if we grant that texts present us with a radical otherness that commands our respect, this command sits uneasily with the nature of interpretation, and thus with the nature of reading. Texts are not self-contained—or if they are, it is only when nobody reads them. To interpret a text just *is* to appropriate it by letting it speak to something in oneself. Of course, we often encounter new and surprising things when we read. But when this happens, it's because our ideas and expectations have changed through the encounter with the text—not because we've put them entirely out of play. If reading truly were "an event that does not correspond to *any* expectations that we might have of it,"[27] it could only take the form of duplicating texts, exactly as they appear. And as Rorty, Schneewind and Skinner ask,

> why do that? We [interpret] because we do not understand the copy of the text we already have. Giving us a second copy will not help. To understand the text just *is* to relate it helpfully to something else. The only question is what that something else will be.[28]

This doesn't mean that there's no difference between reading a text carefully and forcing it to serve a preconceived agenda. On the contrary, it's often easy to distinguish a propagandistic or self-serving reading from one that at least tries to "get the text right." But this is a distinction between two kinds of interpretation, not a distinction between interpretation and something else. To say that readers have a responsibility to preserve the otherness of what they read is to lose sight of how reading works.

A Eudaimonistic Approach

Both the deontological and the alterior approaches try to explain the responsibilities of readers by focusing on *what* we read. They try to derive these responsibilities from the nature of texts—either by seeing texts as a special sort of thing worthy of a special sort of consideration, or by seeing them as the site of an encounter with an otherness that we must not abolish. Since neither of these approaches seems promising, perhaps we should shift our focus away from *what* we read and toward the activity of reading itself. This is the strategy of the third approach I'll consider, which I'll call the *eudaimonistic* approach. Eudaimonistic approaches to ethics claim that the reason we should perform certain actions, or cultivate certain character traits, is that these actions or traits play a crucial role in a life of well-being. The best-known examples are Aristotelian ethical theories, which typically urge us to cultivate certain virtues because these virtues help us attain *eudaimonia*, a state of flourishing sometimes translated as "happiness." For example, Aristotle claims that the reason we should cultivate courage is that courage helps foster eudaimonia, and that eudaimonia is an end at which all human beings naturally aim. This reference to "ends" and "aims" might recall the instrumental approach to norms that I described earlier, but there are two crucial differences. First, for the instrumental approach, norms are means to ends that we merely happen to have. If I want to be a good golfer, I should go to the driving range, but if I don't care about being a good golfer, this "should" loses all force. The instrumental approach is concerned with goals that are optional. A eudaimonistic approach is concerned with non-optional goals, goals that are hardwired into our nature and partly constitutive of what we are. For Aristotle, eudaimonia is not a goal we might or might not pursue. It's a goal we all pursue all the time, and indeed a goal inseparable from our humanity. Second, the instrumental approach is concerned with ends that are externally related to the means that help attain them. A root canal is a means to better teeth, and its value ends there: if I could have better teeth without getting a root canal, I would. Eudaimonistic approaches, by contrast, are concerned with ends that are inseparable from the means used to attain them. According to Aristotle, for instance, courage isn't just an instrument that helps me attain some separate goal called happiness. Rather, a happy life is partly constituted by acts of courage; leading a flourishing life is, in part, being courageous.

At first glance, it's hard to imagine how there could be a eudaimonistic approach to the responsibilities of readers. Unlike the attempt to lead a flourishing life, reading seems optional. We don't have to read; plenty of people don't. So what sense could there be in claiming that readers' responsibilities derive from non-optional goals that are partly constitutive of what they are? To answer this question, I'd like once again to draw on the work of Alasdair MacIntyre, who has argued that eudaimonistic considerations arise in a much wider range of activities than we might first think. MacIntyre's general project is to resurrect Aristotelian ethics by divorcing it from Aristotle's metaphysical biology. MacIntyre doesn't think our final end or our moral obligations can simply be read off from the kinds of animals we are. He focuses instead on the organized social activities that define human beings. The key to his attempt is the concept of a practice, which, as we've seen, he defines as

> any coherent and complex form of socially established cooperative human activity through which goods internal to that form of activity are realized in the course of trying to achieve those standards of excellence which are appropriate to, and partially definitive of, that form of activity, with the result that human powers to achieve excellence, and human conceptions of the ends and goods involved, are systematically extended.[29]

Not every goal-directed activity is a practice. Kicking a ball is not a practice, but playing football is. Hitting a piano key is not a practice, but making music is. Since human beings are social creatures, practices are not exactly optional. There may be no particular practice in which everyone must engage, but all people engage in some practices or other. And once I engage in a practice, there are certain goods I find myself pursuing, simply because they are "appropriate to, and partially definitive of," that practice. Engaging in a practice is inseparable from doing certain things in certain ways.

To highlight the difference between practices and other activities, MacIntyre gives the example of teaching a child to play chess. Suppose I tell a child that if she plays chess with me, I will give her candy. I also tell her that if she wins, she will get even more candy, and that I will play in a way that makes it difficult but not impossible for her to win. At first, the child is motivated solely by her desire for candy. She seeks a good that is external to chess, and chess is nothing more than a means that helps her attain it. She therefore has no reason not to cheat, if she can get away with it. But as we continue to play, there will come a time when the child will find in those goods specific to chess, in the achievement of a certain highly particular kind of analytical skill, strategic imagination and competitive intensity, a new set of reasons, reasons now not just for winning on a particular occasion, but for trying to excel in whatever way the game of chess demands. Now if the child cheats, [she] will be defeating not me, but [herself].[30]

By learning to appreciate the goods internal to chess, the child has become a member of a practice. As a member of that practice, she now has certain responsibilities, such as the responsibility not to cheat. Granted, she might never have started to play chess, and she might never have become fully inculcated into chess as practice. But now that she has been, chess is no longer of merely instrumental value to her. This practice, its internal goods, and its standards of excellence now help constitute who and what she is.

Perhaps we can explain the responsibilities of readers by seeing reading as a practice, in MacIntyre's sense. Perhaps the reason we should read in certain ways rather than others is that reading is an organized activity with internal goods, and by pursuing these goods, we commit ourselves to the standards of excellence that help us attain them. For example, if Jacobs is right about the responsibility to read what brings us genuine joy, perhaps this is because such joy is one of the goods internal to the practice of reading, and that an appreciation of it is like an appreciation of the "strategic imagination and competitive intensity" internal to chess. Perhaps the responsibility to seek joy through reading is like the responsibility chess players have not to cheat: a responsibility first of all *to a practice*, a responsibility one acquires simply by trying to perform a complex activity in a way that's not utterly self-defeating. No doubt some people who read are not fully inculcated into this practice, just as some children play chess simply to win candy. Such people won't really understand why they can't read in any way they like, just as some chess players don't really understand why cheating is wrong. But these are not the people Adler, Jacobs and Woolf are addressing. They are addressing those who see reading as they do—as a pursuit of internal goods through which human powers to achieve excellence are systematically extended. To engage in such a pursuit just *is* to take on certain responsibilities.

Practices, Traditions and History

I believe the eudaimonistic approach, when given this MacIntyrean twist, is the most promising of the three I have considered. Unlike the deontological and alterior approaches, it doesn't have to pin down exactly what a text or an author is. This approach also fits well with readers' reports on their experiences. Many of them draw a sharp distinction between two sorts of readers: those who treat reading as an instrument to be valued for the external goods it brings, and those who read for less obvious, more internal goods. Jacobs, for instance, says that the process of "reading carefully for information in order to upload content" is quite different from the "slow and patient reading [that] properly belongs to our leisure hours."[31] The former is for everyone and should be taught in schools; the latter cannot be taught, but "may, perhaps, only arise from within, according to some inexplicable internal necessity of being."[32] Similarly, as we've seen, Woolf sharply distinguishes those who read for practical or professional purposes from the "common reader" who "is guided by an instinct to create for himself, out of whatever odds and ends he can come by, some kind of whole."[33] The eudaimonistic approach helps explain these distinctions between different sorts of readers who disagree about the value of their activity. But in one respect, MacIntyre's account of practices looks like a poor fit with the experience of reading. Practices, as MacIntyre describes them, are cooperative: organized forms of social life in which different individuals pursue a common good. But reading is usually seen as an individual activity, and an intensely private one at that. As we saw in Chapter 2, many readers describe their activity as a source of pleasurable solitude, a way of retreating from others and learning "how to be alone," to use Franzen's phrase.[34] Does this fact clash with the social nature of practices? How can reading be a practice if it's solitary?

The answer, I think, is that there is no contradiction between the social and the private sides of reading. Reading may let us retreat from others, but retreating from others is a highly specific way of relating to others. The experience of fleeing from one's community and into a book is a well-established way of belonging to that community. I don't just mean that solitary people define themselves in opposition to the groups they flee, though they certainly do. Rather, I mean that to read is to join a community of *other readers*—readers who typically include the very authors one reads. It's a virtual community, most of whose members one will never meet face to face, and many of whose members are no longer alive. But the sense of solidarity that common readers feel toward them is real—as is the sense that the members of this virtual community are engaged in a common practice and pursuing a common good. An example of this attitude appears in a well-known letter from Machiavelli to Francesco Vettori:

> When evening has come, I return to my house and go into my study. At the door I take off my clothes of the day, covered with mud and mire, and I put on my regal and courtly garments; and decently reclothed, I enter the ancient courts of ancient men, where, received by them

lovingly, I feed on the food that alone is mine and that I was born for. There I am not ashamed to speak with them and ask them the reason for their actions; and they in their humanity reply to me. And for the space of four hours I feel no boredom, I forget every pain, I do not fear poverty, death does not frighten me; I deliver myself entirely to them.[35]

Machiavelli's relationship with the ancients displays many of the features of a practice, as MacIntyre describes it. His dialogue with them is a cooperative activity that no individual could complete on her own. Machiavelli relies on their kindness in order to discern "the reason for their actions"; at the same time, the intelligibility of their actions remains hidden unless and until Machiavelli interrogates them. The mutual understanding achieved through this dialogue is a common good not reducible to the sum of individual goods. So are the various internal goods achieved in the course of this pursuit: the dispelling of boredom and fear, the forgetting of trouble and the social bond attained when one gives oneself over to a practice. In the context of a relationship—even a virtual relationship like this one—the responsibilities of readers make sense. Adler's claim that we must hold up our end of the conversation with a book makes sense if readers see themselves as engaged in a cooperative social activity, an activity in which their own flourishing is bound up with the flourishing of their fellow practitioners. The responsibilities of readers make sense if we recognize that reading is social.

It is also historical. As the case of Machiavelli makes clear, practices are not static. They evolve over time, and seeing oneself as a member of a practice involves identifying with earlier members of that practice and knowing at least something about its history. Under favourable conditions, a practice can become what MacIntyre calls a *tradition*, which he characterizes as "a movement in the course of which those engaging in that movement become aware of it and of its direction and in self-aware fashion attempt to engage in its debates and to carry its enquiries forward."[36] When we play chess, in some small way, we enact a new stage in the history of chess. The better a chess player's grasp of the history of her tradition, the better able she is to carry it forward in self-conscious fashion. Similarly, to read is to enact a new stage in the history of the community of readers. The more readers know about the history of this tradition, the better they will understand its possibilities, and the better they will understand the standards of excellence they must respect in order to realize those possibilities. This is not to say that all readers must be historians of reading. But it is to say that the responsibilities of readers are fully intelligible only in context. If I'm right, that context is much bigger than it seems.

Chapter 6

READING THINGS

Here's the Thing

We've now looked at some of the connections between reading and selfhood, and between reading and ethics. In this chapter I'd like to turn to the link between reading and a third philosophical topic: ontology. Ontology, as I'm using the term, is the study of being: an investigation of the things that exist, considered simply *as* things that exist. The question I want to raise is whether the experiences of readers reveal anything about their dealings with things. Does the experience of reading teach us anything about the nature of things as such, or about the roles that things play in our lives? To be clear, I'm not suggesting that reading or the study of it are ways of solving metaphysical problems on the cheap. I'm not suggesting that reflecting on reading will yield straightforward solutions to the sorites paradox or the problem of the one and the many. And I'm certainly not suggesting that the experiences of readers give them privileged insights into the nature of reality—that a voracious reader knows more than anyone else about what really exists as opposed to what merely appears to. What interests me is the possibility that readers' experiences shed light on the *meanings* that things have for us. After all, reading is a way of encountering things that matter to us: namely, books and the other things that we read.[1] Perhaps reflecting on the ways in which these things matter to readers will reveal something about the ways in which things more generally matter to us. This is an ontological question, but it's a question for a *descriptive* ontology, since it concerns how we do, in fact, understand things, rather than with how a scientist or a philosopher would say we ought to understand them. It could also be called a question for a *hermeneutical* ontology, since it's concerned with the meanings of things rather than the sheer fact of them.

All of this must sound hopelessly ambitious. Any attempt to reflect on the meanings of things raises a great many thorny issues. For one thing, the meanings of things, and particularly the things we read, emerge under highly specific social and historical conditions and vary tremendously from one setting to another. That books matter to contemporary Westerners in the precise ways they do has a great deal to do with contingent developments, such as the roles books have played in the three Abrahamic religious traditions. Similarly, that Westerners tend to read silently rather than aloud is a contingent historical development, and so is their closely related tendency to associate reading with experiences of privacy and interiority.[2] It's also clear that the meanings books have for us are conditioned by the technologies we use to read. They presuppose technologies of handwriting, of producing paper, of printing, storing and distributing physical books, and increasingly, of making texts appear on electronic screens. Economic conditions also play a role, since the things we read acquire the meanings they do only amid certain forms of production and consumption. A book can't mean anything to me unless I have access to it, and that usually requires that I have the money to buy it or that my community has built and maintained a library from which I can borrow it.[3] It also presupposes that I have time and leisure in which to read the book, and that the author was able to support herself as she wrote it. The question I'm raising in this chapter—what do the things we read mean to us?—can't be easily uncoupled from any of these larger issues. I won't be able to make more than the most cursory remarks about them. But my wager is that there are still worthwhile things to be said about reading's ontological side, even if they're far from the last word.

Taking my cue from the reports of common readers, I'm going to advance two related claims about the ontology of reading. First, readers typically experience books and the other things they read as ontologically dual: as displaying two very different, and indeed opposed, sorts of being. They experience them both as particular physical objects and as things that are not obviously particular physical items—something that, for lack of a better term, might be called a *virtual* entity. My copy of *Madame Bovary* is a particular physical thing, an object on one of my shelves. But this object is also a vessel for something distinct from it, something we might call the *content* of *Madame Bovary*, or *Madame Bovary* "itself." This content is instantiated in my copy, but also in every other copy of the book, and it could be instantiated in indefinitely many more. My copy of *Madame Bovary* is one object among others; its content, as Georges Poulet puts it, is experienced as "no longer just an object," but rather something like "a consciousness."[4] My particular copy of *Madame Bovary* can be destroyed, but *Madame Bovary* itself, it seems, cannot be—not even if *every* copy of it vanishes. The term "book" is therefore ambiguous, since it names both of these things: both particular physical copies of *Madame Bovary* and the virtual content expressed by these copies. Both are real, but not in the same way.

My second claim is that each of these things—physical object and virtual content—can in turn matter to readers in two different and opposed ways.

Each can be encountered as something that matters to us *instrumentally*, because of what we can *do* with it, or as something that matters *intrinsically, in itself*, independently of the uses to which we might put it. Each can be encountered as something like a tool, something we can use to advance our own particular purposes, or as, so to speak, a "mere" thing—something whose significance is not exhausted by those purposes. I will use the term *collecting* to refer to the latter way of relating to books—books in the sense of contents as well as in the sense of copies. It may sound odd to speak of collecting a book's content, since this content doesn't have a spatiotemporal location and cannot, say, be placed on a shelf. But part of my goal here is to argue that it does make sense to speak of collecting contents in this way—even though it's hard at first to see what this might mean.

In short, when we examine the experiences of common readers, we find four distinct ways of relating to books, four different ways in which books can matter to us. We can encounter books as particular physical objects valued for what they can do for us, as particular physical objects valued for their own sakes, as virtual contents valued for what they can do for us and as virtual contents valued for their own sakes. Perhaps some of these types of mattering are more widespread than the others. Clearly some of them have been more widely discussed than the others. But I suspect that none should be seen as more fundamental than any of the others. None of them captures what books *really*, at bottom, are, and none of them captures the way in which books *really*, at bottom, matter. There just isn't a single answer to the questions of what books are and why they matter. In our dealings with books, we encounter different kinds of things that matter in fundamentally different ways.

What does any of this have to do with the larger concerns of philosophy? What interests me about this fragmented way of encountering things is that it isn't unique to reading. Analogues of it can be found in other spheres, including several that many people care about a great deal. But reading presents a particularly clear version of it, a particularly accessible route to an important lesson: that things, considered *as* things, can simultaneously have radically different and opposed meanings for us. The meanings of things can be multiple, in tension, perhaps even contradictory. When readers reflect on the ways books matter to them, they're presented with an especially clear version of this ontological lesson. I want to suggest that one of the reasons reading matters so much to so many people is that it lets them experience and reflect on the fragmentation built into their encounters with things. This reflection usually isn't fully explicit. It may be more dimly sensed than thematized. And it certainly doesn't solve the puzzle of how what seems to be one and the same thing can display radically different sorts of being and matter in radically different ways. But it *shows* readers this puzzle, and helps them recognize it *as a puzzle*.

Reading confronts them with what Gabriel Marcel called "the mystery of being."[5]

First, though, let me anticipate an objection. The way I've framed the issue assumes that there is something general to say about things and our dealings with them—that the question "what do things mean to us?" has a non-vacuous answer. One might think that it doesn't. Perhaps things and the ways in which we relate to them are too varied for generalizations like these. Even if we restrict our focus to books, perhaps they vary so much that they resist generalization: different books can have very different meanings, even to a single reader. So perhaps there is nothing informative to say about the things we read as such—let alone things as such—or the meanings they have for us. And if there isn't, then the questions I've raised might not admit of an answer, or at least not an interesting one. But while it's undeniable that things and their meanings vary enormously, it doesn't follow that there is no room for generalizations here. That a concept is extremely general doesn't mean that there is nothing informative to say about it. Philosophers have, after all, managed to say a great deal about what *actions* are, and *texts*, and *historical events*. All of these concepts are exceedingly general, and their instances vary enormously. Some philosophers have even found it fruitful to reflect on the concepts of *being* and of a *thing*, though these concepts are as abstract, and as hard to generalize about, as any concepts can be. Aristotle had quite a bit to say about the features displayed by all beings *qua* beings; Heidegger managed to say quite a bit about the major kinds of things and their most general features.[6] We might not accept everything—or anything—that Aristotle and Heidegger say about the nature of things, or that other philosophers have said about the nature of actions, texts or historical events. The point is simply that the projects in which these philosophers are engaged are not obviously pointless or doomed to failure. Clearly, there are pitfalls in any enterprise that requires a lot of generalizing. But the pitfalls don't mean that the enterprise can't succeed, and they are not a reason not to make the attempt.

Relating to Books

Let me start by taking a quick look at two well-known essays written by common readers: Walter Benjamin's "Unpacking My Library" and George Orwell's "Bookshop Memories." Both texts describe two different ways of relating to books, and the distinctions they draw will help focus our discussion of the ontology of reading. In "Unpacking My Library," Benjamin distinguishes two ways in which his book collection might be considered valuable. One emphasizes the books' "usefulness," their "functional, utilitarian value."[7] Seen in this way, the books have value as instruments, as tools that contribute to specific projects. What matters about the books from this perspective are "their usefulness to a writer"[8] or other professionals, and *only* their usefulness to such people. To those who view books in this way, having books and not putting them to use is just as perverse as owning nice china and not eating off of it.[9] But it's also possible to view books in a way that stresses something other than their utilitarian value. From this other perspective, books appear as mere objects and are valued for their own sakes—or perhaps, as Benjamin suggestively puts it, as "the scene, the stage, of their fate."[10] Benjamin calls this the attitude of the collector, and for the collector, the acquisition of books amounts to "the locking of individual items within a magic circle."[11] Collecting is in tension with usefulness. When a book is locked away in a collection, it becomes less "useful academically" and thus more "objectionable socially."[12] But to the true collector, all of this is beside the point. The point is for "the objects [to] get their due,"[13] and this happen only when our normal ways of using the objects are suspended.

Orwell draws a similar distinction while describing his experiences of working in a bookshop. Before taking the job, he says, "I really did love books. [...] Nothing pleased me quite so much as to buy a job lot of them for a shilling at a country auction."[14] Orwell's love of books was initially linked to what they allowed him to do. Books are perfect, he says, for when you want to be soothed or distracted, "in your bath, for instance, or late at night when you are too tired to go to bed, or in the odd quarter of an hour before lunch."[15] But once Orwell was obliged to be around large numbers of books much of the time, he started to encounter them another way—as mere things, as objects. He did not find this change pleasant:

> As soon as I went to work in the bookshop I stopped buying books. Seen in the mass, five or ten thousand at a time, books were boring and even slightly sickening. Nowadays I do buy one occasionally, but only if it is a book that I want to read and can't borrow, and I never buy junk. The sweet smell of decaying paper appeals to me no longer.[16]

Orwell's disgust at books in the mass is reminiscent of a famous scene from Jean-Paul Sartre's novel *Nausea*, where Antoine Roquentin has a frightening encounter with the root of a chestnut tree, losing his ability to relate to it as a root, confronting it simply as an existing thing: as "a black, knotty mass, entirely beastly."[17] In a similar way, overfamiliarity causes Orwell's usual grip on books to loosen. Having lost the ability to relate to them as equipment, he is forced to confront them as mere things.

Though their attitudes differ—one delights in the way books can be appreciated as objects, while the other is sickened by it—Benjamin and Orwell are drawing a similar distinction. Both distinguish the stance in which we use books from the stance in which we relate to them as objects. Both distinguish a stance in which books are treated as instruments to be integrated into our projects from a stance in which they are treated as things we possess or collect. In the former stance, we see books as tools with which to do something in particular. In the latter stance, we see them simply as things, things whose meaning and interest go beyond any particular function they might serve for us. Of course, this distinction isn't perfectly sharp. I doubt that the possession of books can ever be totally divorced from instrumental considerations. As Jean Baudrillard has noted, collectors are often passionate people whose collections meet powerful psychological needs.[18] Still, it's useful to distinguish between a relatively interest-driven way of encountering books, and a relatively disinterested way of doing so—even if the boundary between these activities is fuzzy.

Distinctions like this have always been a staple of the writings of common readers. They're often used to criticize those who care more about owning books than about reading them—those, in other words, who allow a book's character as an object to crowd out its usefulness as a tool. An early example is Lucian of Samosata, whose second-century tract "Remarks Addressed to an Illiterate Book-Fancier" mocks wealthy collectors who think they can master a book's contents simply by buying a physical copy of it. Lucian counters that the true book lover is one who "derives benefit" from what he reads, either by learning to express himself better or by improving his character through exposure to the great. When a book owner fails to profit from his possessions in this way, "what are his books but a habitation for mice and vermin, and a source of castigation to negligent servants?"[19] Another well-known example—and the first recorded use of the term "bibliomania"—is a letter from the fourth Earl of Chesterfield to his book-collecting son. The Earl advises his son to "buy good books, and read them," adding that "the best books are the commonest, and the last editions are always the best, if the editors are not blockheads."[20] The distinction between physical books and their contents also pops up frequently in advice about how to read. Mortimer Adler tells readers to mark up their books with no concern about damaging them. "Full ownership of a book," Adler says, "only comes when you have made it a part of yourself, and the best way to make yourself a part of it—which comes to the same thing—is by writing in it."[21] According to Adler, treating a book as an object that mustn't be sullied through use only obscures its real meaning.

But not all common readers subordinate ownership to use in this way. Some do the reverse, prizing the physical copies they collect more than their contents. Carter Burden speaks for many serious book collectors when he says "I love to read my books, but I also enjoy them as objects. I like living with them. I like holding them [...] I like putting books where they belong."[22] What matters to

Burden isn't just owning the titles he does, but dealing with them as objects. "Not having the books around is distressing," he says, and "to collect abstractly from a catalogue, without being able to handle them, is not collecting."[23] In extreme cases, collectors care so much about their books' thingly character that they're hostile to the very idea of using them. Joe Queenan reports that his daughter hates libraries, which she thinks involve "everything bad about cemeteries without any of the redeeming qualities."[24] To Queenan's daughter, valuing usefulness over ownership isn't just a mistake, but a sign of a vicious character. "If you don't want to own books," she says, "it means you are an asshole."[25] Perhaps the most extreme version of this attitude is displayed by bibliomaniacs who amass huge collections by stealing from libraries. Stephen Blumberg and John Gilkey each stole thousands of books despite having no practical use for them and only the vaguest idea of their contents.[26] Blumberg and Gilkey probably come as close as it's possible to go to valuing books purely as objects.[27] But I suspect that most serious readers have at least a little sympathy for both the user and the collector. They may identify more closely with one attitude than the other, but they probably think that each is on to something. Books really do matter both intrinsically and instrumentally.

One might think that the distinction between collecting books and using them corresponds to another distinction I've mentioned: the distinction between physical copies of books and their virtual contents. We might assume that collecting is something one does with the physical copies of books, while using is something one does with their contents. But the reality is messier. Both the physical copies of books and their contents can be valued in each of the ways I've outlined. A physical copy can be valued both as an object to be collected and as a tool to be used. After all, not all ways of using books concern their contents. Their physical copies can also be useful in all sorts of ways—by saving me a trip to the library, for instance, or even by serving as a doorstopper. Similarly, a book's content can be valued both as an object to be possessed and as an instrument with which to do things. It's not hard to see how readers might use the things they've read. They might acquire new beliefs and act on them, or engage emotionally with the contents of books. It's harder to see how they might collect the contents of books, given that these contents are virtual rather than physical. But in fact, readers do this all the time. Readers take pleasure in the fact they have read this or that book, even if they care little about physical copies. Such readers are still collecting, but they're collecting something other than physical objects. They're collecting *readings* of books, and deriving satisfaction from the fact that they've had the experience of reading these works.

At first, one might think that a reading of *Madame Bovary* is an entirely separate thing than the content of *Madame Bovary* itself. But the relation between the two is actually more complicated. As Peter Kivy has argued, a reading of *Madame Bovary* is a *token* of *Madame Bovary* itself, while *Madame Bovary* itself is the *type* of which it is a token.[28] Just as a performance of Beethoven's fifth symphony is distinct from the symphony itself—the former is a particular event with a spatiotemporal location, while the latter is not—a reading of *Madame Bovary* is distinct from *Madame Bovary* itself. But just as the performance instantiates the symphony, the reading instantiates the book. Kivy puts a distinctive spin on this claim, arguing that readings just are a kind of performance. They are, he claims, private, inner experiences in which one enacts a text for oneself in much the same way that a public reading enacts a text for an audience. But it's not necessary to accept all the details of Kivy's position to accept his key point. The point is simply that it makes sense to speak of readers collecting the contents of books, although these contents are not particular physical objects. The content is a type; a reading of the book is a token of that type; and one collects readings by having experiences of a certain kind.

How common is it for readers to collect readings in this way—for the sake of doing so, rather than out of some particular interest? No doubt some cases of collecting that initially look disinterested are really driven by a disguised interest. The person who reads all the books she can because she hopes others will learn about her reading and admire her for it is an obvious example.[29] But there do seem to be cases in which readers genuinely collect readings for their own sake. Consider the case of Pamela Paul. Since she was a teenager, Paul has kept a list of the books she's read, calling it Bob (for "Book of Books"). But Bob doesn't just give her material to brag about or allow her to feel cultured. Quite the reverse: flipping through Bob is a humbling, painful experience for her, because it reminds her of all the books she's read of which she remembers nothing. What's more, when she tells people about Bob, they usually react negatively: "'You're tallying up books like the ticking off of accomplishments,' one ex-boyfriend accused me, as if I'd admitted to quantifying parental love or indexing my inner beauty. 'Hurry, go note it in Bob,' he'd gibe every time I closed a book."[30] But none of this disapproval lessens Paul's "satisfaction at the growing tally."[31] Some of this satisfaction comes from Bob's usefulness as an autobiographical tool. It helps her preserve what she was thinking about at various points in her life, and trace changes in her tastes. But a larger part has to do with the intrinsic satisfaction of amassing readings. Just as Carter Burden values his physical books as objects, Paul values the texts she's read as things to be collected, even though the collecting in question is virtual.

I'll have more to say about the ontology of collecting readings shortly. For now, I'd like to note something about the very idea of collecting books, whether physical tokens or virtual copies. Since at least the appearance of Kant's *Critique of Judgment*, it's been common for philosophers to claim that most of our dealings with things are interest-driven: attempts to use the thing for some particular purpose. The pleasure we take in food or sleep, for example, is interested in that it satisfies specific physical appetites. The pleasure we take in being admired, or attractive, or good at our jobs, is interested in less obvious but equally real ways. Kant argues that the experience of the beautiful offers a respite from these interest-driven ways of relating to things. The beautiful, he claims, pleases without interest: it is a pleasure not based on what the beautiful thing can do for us. It's striking that when common readers discuss the collecting of books, they often speak of a similar suspension of utilitarian considerations. When Benjamin speaks of giving objects their due, and when Paul speaks of her satisfaction at her growing tally of readings, they claim to be relating to books in a way that disrupts their usual, interested dealings with things. In that way, they claim to be experiencing a shift in what things mean to them. Something that's genuinely useful, something that usually gets its meaning from its utility as an instrument, undergoes a change in aspect, and is encountered as a thing in its own right. A shift of this sort seems to be what Alan Jacobs has in mind when he says that a good book "asks us to change our lives by putting aside what we usually think of as good reasons. It's asking us to stop calculating."[32] Of course, it's possible that when readers think they're relating to their books in an interest-free way, they're mistaken. Perhaps what they take to be a disinterested relation with books is really driven by some other, hidden interest. But even if their experience is deluded, there has still been a shift *in their experience*. And if we're concerned with what the things we read mean to us, then the character of that experience can't be ignored.

Still, it's significant that what seems to be happening in such cases is a *shift* in what books mean to readers. Either a physical book or its content goes from being experienced as a tool to be used to being experienced as an object to be collected, or the reverse. That there can be such shifts suggests that there's an instability at the heart of the things we read. Rather than being simply useful tools or collectable objects, they can be experienced as one or the other. Moreover, they tend to slip from one to the other, being encountered under different aspects over the course of our dealings with them. No matter how disinterested a type of pleasure seems, it's not hard to make a case that it also involves some hidden interest. And no matter how pure my love for the thingly character of my books seems, it's hard not to wonder whether some unconscious interest lies at its source. Conversely, no matter how instrumental my relationship with a thing seems, it's hard to imagine it involving *no* recognition of its status as a mere object. A purely instrumental relationship to a tool would have to be totally frictionless, with the tool never resisting our purposes by breaking down or failing to do what we want. It's just as hard to imagine anyone having a purely instrumental relationship with the books she reads, a relationship in which the books' status as mere things plays no role whatsoever. For all these reasons, it seems better to speak of disruptions or interruptions in the meanings books have for someone than to speak of someone simply valuing a book as an instrument or as an object. One of these meanings may dominate in a given context, but it's plausible that both are present to some degree.

All of this suggests that it's unwise to ask what books *really* mean to readers, as though one of these meanings were genuine and the other mere appearance. On the contrary, the most salient fact about the meanings of books is their bifurcated quality: the way books seesaw from being objects to being tools, and back again. Indeed, a concern with both aspects of books' meaning is a widespread feature of the reports of common readers. Consider "Unpacking My Library" again. For all his talk of giving objects their due, the fact is that Benjamin collects books rather than stamps or cookie jars. Surely part of the reason he values these objects so much is that for him, they're *not* just objects. What they mean to him is inseparable from the ways they can be used in practices of reading and writing. In fact, when we encounter people who come close to valuing books as mere objects, we tend to find them strange and a little creepy. The person who collects books as an investment or because they look nice in his living room strikes us as an oddball or a philistine, not a gifted closet metaphysician. Orwell was vaguely outraged when he started working in a bookshop and discovered "the rarity of really bookish people."[33] Or consider the attitude of many Canadians to retail chain Chapters, which, since 1994, has dominated the country's book industry. Lots of people dislike Chapters, and one of the things they dislike most is that when the company was created, none of its founders had any real experience with books. They were, in the words of one commentator, "just a bunch of venture capitalists looking for an industry to take over."[34] The hostility that some Canadians feel toward Chapters suggests that we *expect* people to recognize and respect the different ways in which books matter. That the meanings of books are multiple isn't an obscure philosophical lesson, but one of the most basic facts about the practice of reading.

This chapter began with a question: what do books mean to readers? It seems that the simplest answer to this question is that they mean several things, and these different meanings are in tension. It would be naïve to try to resolve this tension. As we've just seen, readers typically recognize that this tension exists, and while their particular interests may lead them to privilege one pole of the tension over the other, they're remarkably unconcerned with doing away with it. A big part of the interest of reading seems to stem from the way it lets readers relate to things in opposed ways simultaneously, without insisting that one of these ways is more real than the other. If reading matters a great deal to people, this may help explain why.

Collecting the Virtual

If what I've said so far is on the right track, then there is reason to think readers can and sometimes do collect readings as well as physical books. But the nature of this sort of collecting is still hazy. What is it like to collect readings, and what kinds of things must readings be in order to be capable of being collected? Although these sound like very obscure questions, a recent exploration of them became a surprise international bestseller: Pierre Bayard's *How to Talk about Books You Haven't Read*. Bayard doesn't exactly set out to contribute to ontology. His book is more a piece of cultural critique. It describes an attitude toward books and reading that has become dominant in some circles; argues that this attitude is unhealthy; and sketches an alternative that Bayard believes is healthier. But the key premises of Bayard's argument concern ontological matters. As he sees it, the problem with the dominant attitude toward books and reading is that it misunderstands the sort of things books are. This attitude prizes readings and urges us to possess them, but since it misunderstands the nature of these readings, it overstates the degree to which possessing them is possible. Moreover, the alternative that Bayard defends is to be preferred largely because it has a better understanding of what books are, and of the ways they resist our attempts to control them. In other words, it rests on a better ontology. For all these reasons, *How to Talk about Books You Haven't Read* helps illuminate what it means to collect readings, even though doing so is not its main agenda.

The target of *How to Talk about Books You Haven't Read* is a certain fetishization of books and reading. "We still live in a society," Bayard writes, "where reading remains the object of a kind of worship."[35] The "society" he has in mind here is evidently quite narrow. A professor of literature at the University of Paris, Bayard seems to have in mind French academic and literary circles. He describes a milieu in which, to be considered a cultivated person, it is necessary to have read certain books and to be able to express views about them. In this milieu, being cultivated is equated with possessing cultural literacy, and cultural literacy is a matter of having certain books at one's fingertips. But the books that are expected to be at one's fingertips are clearly not physical books. One gets no credit in Bayard's circles for owning a handsome or extensive library. One is rather expected to have mastered the contents of these books. What's more, one is expected to have mastered these contents regardless of their usefulness for any particular project. In Bayard's circles, to ask what all this reading is good for, to ask about the uses of culture, is to betray the most boorish *lack* of cultivation. There is an obvious parallel here with the idea of the liberal arts, originally conceived as arts suitable for free men—men wealthy enough not to have to use their knowledge to earn a living. Similarly, in the milieu Bayard describes, cultural literacy is seen as having intrinsic value. One doesn't read Shakespeare or Proust in order to do anything in particular. At most, being familiar with them is a "matter of *orientation*. Being cultivated is a matter not of having read any book in particular, but of being able to find your bearings within books as a system."[36] The point of internalizing a literary culture in this way is to be able to steer one's way through that culture. To try to exploit one's familiarity with culture in some other sphere is to miss the point.

But what are these things that one must possess in order to be cultivated? Bayard's explicitly ontological claims can sound strange: he says, for example, that "a book is not limited to itself,"[37] and that a book we have read is really "an anomalous accumulation of fragments of texts, reworked by our imagination and unrelated to the books of others."[38] He is clearer about these matters when he describes the practices of talking about books that are central to being considered a cultivated person. These practices, he argues, require that we distinguish three different senses of "book," three different objects that figure in conversations about books. The first is a "screen book," which Bayard characterizes as "an imaginary object based on [one's] own personal agenda."[39] A screen book consists of "what the reader knows or believes about the book,"[40] and since one can believe things about books one hasn't even seen, screen books can be largely fabricated. As an example, Bayard cites the missing second volume of Aristotle's *Poetics*, a book about which nearly nothing is known, but which is central to the plot of Umberto Eco's novel *Foucault's Pendulum*. Next is the "inner book," defined as "the set of mythic representations, be they collective or individual, that come between the reader and any new piece of writing, shaping his reading without his realizing it."[41] A reader's inner book is a sort of interpretive schema, a set of unconscious expectations that "acts as a filter and determines the reception of new texts by selecting which of its elements will be retained and how they will be interpreted."[42] It includes fairly specific assumptions about the nature of texts—for example, that they make up unified wholes—as well as all the other beliefs with which the things we read must cohere. Screen books are therefore constructed on the basis of inner books. My ideas about the second book of the *Poetics* are constrained by my assumptions about what philosophy texts are usually like and about what sort of thinker Aristotle is. Finally, Bayard uses the term "phantom book" to name "that mobile and ungraspable object that we call into being, in writing or in speech, when we talk about a book."[43] A phantom book "is located at the point where readers' various *screen books* meet."⁴⁴ It is a collective achievement, a socially shared set of meanings. In Bayard's subculture, a mutable but relatively stable set of associations is evoked by terms like *Eugenie Grandet* or *Hamlet*. These shared meanings are what we are talking about when we talk about these titles. The details of this shared understanding constrain what one can and can't say about them. Nothing but scorn awaits those who can't talk about *Hamlet* at all, or whose ways of talking about it veer too much from what the rest of us have come to expect.

None of these books—screen books, inner books or phantom books—are physical things. Yet each can be collected. I can collect all sorts of screen books, in that I can have my own ideas about indefinitely many titles—even if these ideas are largely wrong. I'm also free to collect all manner of inner books. My inner books are simply the assumptions that steer me to interpret new texts in one way rather than another. These assumptions aren't infinitely flexible, but they can vary quite a bit, and there's no obvious limit to the tweaking and refining I can do to them. Finally, and most importantly, it's possible to collect phantom books. Possessing a phantom book is simply a matter of being able to talk in socially sanctioned ways about certain shared meanings. My ability to do this is limited only by how much time and energy I have to become familiar with different titles and convince other people that I understand them. The number of phantom books with which I can become familiar is extremely large, because according to Bayard, I can talk about a book in the socially required ways even if I haven't cast my eyes over a physical copy. "Being cultivated," Bayard says,

> is a matter not of having read any book in particular, but of being able to find your bearings within books as a system, which requires you to know that they form a system and to be able to locate each element in relation to the others. The interior of the book is less important than its exterior, or, if you prefer, the interior of the book *is* its exterior, since what counts in a book is the books alongside it.⁴⁵

It's possible, therefore, "to speak with relative precision [...] about a book one has never held in one's hands."⁴⁶ And since the capacity to talk about books isn't acquired for any higher purpose—as we've seen, to ask what culture is for is to betray a lack of culture—it's a matter of collecting rather than use.

In fact, we can go even further than Bayard does. Not only is it possible to collect all three sorts of books; it seems inevitable that all three will be collected together. In Bayard's scheme, the sort of book that readers care most about collecting is the phantom book, the shared set of meanings that is the object of one's conversations with other readers. According to this scheme, to be cultivated is to share plenty of phantom books—and the right phantom books—with one's conversational partners. But while Bayard doesn't explicitly say so, a little reflection suggests that one can't collect phantom books without also collecting screen books and inner books. A phantom book, after all, is simply the intersection among various readers' screen books. You and I share a phantom book when two of our screen books overlap. But our screen books can't overlap unless we both have them in the first place. We can collect phantom books, therefore, only when we collect the relevant screen books. And inner books, as we've seen, are simply the assumptions or interpretive schemata that mediate our access to books—specific assumptions about specific books, but also general assumptions about all books. In order to collect a certain screen book, I must collect the relevant inner book: that is, I must have certain assumptions that give me access to that book. We can collect screen books, therefore, only when we collect the relevant inner books. In Bayard's scheme, to talk about books is in the first instance to collect phantom books. But to collect phantom books is to collect the other two sorts as well.

Bayard's goal, as we've seen, is to criticize his culture's attitude toward books. But what he criticizes isn't the very idea of collecting readings. There's nothing intrinsically problematic about a culture that prizes the possession of phantom books, as manifested in the ability to discuss them in certain ways. What Bayard finds problematic is his culture's assumptions about how successful these enterprises can be. He argues that his culture equates collecting books with a perfect mastery of them. According to this ideal, to have read a book is to possess it completely, such that all of its details are fully and forever at one's disposal. But this is an impossible ideal. The problem is not just that it's hard to read all the books one is expected to, or to read them as carefully as one is expected to. No matter how hard one tries, possession of a book can only ever be partial and fleeting. Even the most careful forms of reading are in a constant, losing battle with forgetting. "After being read," Bayard argues, "a book immediately begins to disappear from consciousness, to the point where it becomes impossible to remember whether we have read it."[47] Many of us have had the experience of reading a book for what we think is the first time, only to come across marginal notes we made during an earlier reading.[48] Montaigne reputedly failed to recognize passages from his own books when they were read to him. If the mark of having read a book is full possession, don't we have to say, absurdly, that Montaigne hadn't read his own books? Shouldn't we instead reject "the fantasy that there exists such a thing as thorough reading,"[49] and agree with Bayard that "the content of a text is so fluid that it is difficult to ascertain with certainty that something is not found in it?"[50]

Bayard caught a lot of flak after publishing *How to Talk about Books You Haven't Read*. Some made him out to be a postliterate barbarian. Novelist

Jay McInerney, for instance, claimed that "in Bayard's nonreading utopia the printing press would never have been invented, let alone penicillin or the MacBook."[51] Few of these critics noticed that his claims were far more subtle than his book's provocative title suggested. Few noticed, for example, that far from advising his readers to talk about books they hadn't read, Bayard suggests that the very idea of doing so makes little sense.[52] Be that as it may, Bayard makes a number of useful suggestions about what it means to collect the contents of books, rather than physical copies of them. First, he suggests that there is nothing mysterious about such collecting. The objects collected through this activity need not be understood as peculiar, immaterial things. What is being collected are simply *readings*: the experience of having read certain books, an experience manifest in the ability to talk in certain ways about what one has read. Granted, Bayard's account leaves a number of questions unanswered. In Kivy's terms, a reading of *Madame Bovary* is a token, and the type of which it *is* a token—*Madame Bovary* itself—is a mysterious entity that is not at all easy to characterize. It's easier to describe negatively than positively: it is not, for example, a transcription of *Madame Bovary*, much less a particular copy of that transcription. But while it's hard to say anything positive about what this type is, the same is true of other types with familiar tokens. It's difficult to say precisely what pain, or fear, or Beethoven's fifth symphony is, other than by contrasting them with their tokens. The contrast is relatively straightforward, even if the nature of one of its terms is not. Finally, and perhaps most importantly, Bayard suggests that collecting readings needn't involve an unqualified possession of them. We need not, and should not, think that to collect a reading of a book means that one has total mastery over it. According to Bayard, we *never* master books in this way; our grasp over our readings is never more than partial and fleeting. If we define cultivation in terms of the collection of readings, we must concede that it can be difficult or impossible to say whether we've collected a given reading or not.

Collecting Writ Large

All of this must sound terribly rarified. Most people aren't serious book collectors, and those who are usually don't have elaborate metaphysical theories about their collections. So even if it's possible to use the things we read as a route to ontological insights, why should we think that large numbers of people will be interested in this phenomenon? Even if our encounters with books do show that things can possess several incompatible meanings at once, why is this lesson relevant to anyone but people like Benjamin and Bayard—belletristic intellectuals whose concerns are distant from those of most common readers?

Here I have to repeat a claim that I've made many times. It's certainly true that explicit reflection on the ontological status of books is an uncommon and highly rarified activity. But like other forms of philosophical reflection, it gets its interest and its legitimacy from the way it articulates issues that a great many people care about—perhaps in ways that are only semi-explicit or confused. We've seen this with the topics of selfhood and morality. Most people don't reflect on these topics as explicitly or as doggedly as professional philosophers do in their journal articles and seminar rooms. But if these professional treatments are interesting, it's because they express concerns about what selves are and how one ought to live that are quite widespread. The ontological questions raised by Benjamin, Orwell and Bayard are similar. They are intensely focused versions of the much more general question of what things mean to us. And the lesson they teach—namely, that a pervasive feature of things is their ability to display several opposed meanings at once—is compelling because it's a view to which we're driven in a great many contexts, in our dealings with a great many type of things. After all, it's quite common to notice that one and the same thing seems to display two radically different natures—almost as if it were two completely different things. It's only natural to be puzzled by this fragmentation, and quite a few classic philosophical problems are attempts to come to terms with this sort of puzzlement. Consider the sorts of difficulties we encounter when we think about what human beings are. As Thomas Nagel has pointed out, we often find ourselves oscillating between an "external" or "objective" perspective and an "internal" or "subjective" perspective on ourselves.[53] We sometimes view a human being as a certain kind of animal, an object best described in the third-person language of natural science. But we also view a human being as "a particular person inside the world"[54]—a subject who acts, values and experiences in a way that can be understood only from a first-person perspective. Neither of these perspectives seems illusory. Both the objective and subjective perspectives seem to reveal human beings as they are, though the prospects of reconciling them in a single vision look dim. A human being, we want to say, is actually several incompatible things at once—but *how* it can have these incompatible natures is a mystery. Similar observations are sometimes made about art works. We encounter a work of art as both a thing among things and as somehow more than a thing—or, as Robert Pippin puts it, as "both as itself an object and as resistant, in manifold ways, to such objectification."[55] Surely this is part of what Heidegger had in mind when he characterized the work of art as a "strife" between "world" and "earth."[56] Genuine art works involve a dynamic tension between the horizons of meaning that they disclose and the physical materials that make them up. In a successful work, neither overwhelms the other; indeed, each needs the other. A Van Gogh painting of peasant shoes is both a revelation of the peasant's world and mere blobs of paint on a canvas. In our dealings with things, we can't help but have some dim sense of what the things in question are. But in the case of human beings, art works and perhaps many other sorts of things, there doesn't seem to be just one answer to the question of what they are. The things seem to be fragmented and multiple, with several incompatible ways of being, and we can't see how to bring them together. We can't stop seeing both as real, but we can't understand how both *can* be real. Their existence presents us with a puzzle.

My hunch is that one of the reasons common readers are fascinated by their dealings with books is that books offer an especially clear site for thinking through this puzzle. Like human beings and art works, books seem to be several different things at once. They are both physical objects and virtual contents, and what's more, they have both intrinsic and instrumental value. The tension between these aspects is so great that it's not clear how they can all be real—just as it's not clear how a human being can be both an object in nature and a site of experiences that are essentially first-person. But our encounters with books are a sphere in which we have a well-developed practice for dealing with these different sides: the practice of *collecting*. As Benjamin points out, the collecting of physical copies is a familiar and established practice with its own norms and internal goods. But so, as Bayard shows, is the practice of collecting readings and talking about them in socially sanctioned ways. To be sure, there are tensions in these practices, and some of their goals—complete and permanent mastery of a book's contents, for instance—may be unattainable or even incoherent. The point is that when we collect books, we are no longer simply at the mercy of their contradictions. We are engaged in organized attempt to bring order to their mysteries.

In short, the collecting of books and readings might be the best example we have of a practice that acknowledges and tries to integrate the different, opposed sides of things. It doesn't solve all the problems that arise from the recognition that a thing can exhibit several different natures at once. But it *shows* us these problems, and above all, it shows us the *difficulty* of these problems. Even when this practice devolves into pathological forms—the bibliomania of Blumberg and Gilkey, or the fetishization of literary culture that Bayard describes—it points out something valuable about the things that surround us. It reminds us that our attempts to impose order on things, and to hold the different aspects of things in a single vision, can never be more than partial and incomplete. In short, the practice of collecting reminds us that things are a problem for us, and that to some degree, we must be content to let the problem remain a problem.

Collecting the Collectors

Ontology is always abstract, since it deals with the most general features of things: the features they have simply *because* they are things. So it's not surprising that this chapter has been an exceptionally abstract one, devoted to reflections on the most general characteristics of the things we read. For that reason, it might be helpful to end the chapter on a slightly less abstract note. It might be helpful to illustrate some of the claims I've made in this chapter, by giving a concrete example of what it's like for readers to engage in the sorts of ontological reflection I've described. So to bring the chapter to a close, I'd like to give a brief rereading of one of the texts mentioned at its beginning: Benjamin's "Unpacking My Library." The reader giving this reading is, of course, me, and the preoccupations brought to it are mine and mine alone. But on the assumption that my experiences as a reader might share something with those of others, I'd like to show three things. First, when we view Benjamin's text through an explicitly ontological lens, it becomes clear that collecting is a way of coming to terms with the distinct types of being displayed by the things we read. Second, the collector, as presented by Benjamin, is only partly successful at bringing these oppositions into a harmonious whole—which is exactly what we'd expect, given how intractable these oppositions are. Third, those of us who read Benjamin, *by our very reading* of his ontological reflections, nevertheless manage to bring a kind of order to them. Benjamin's collector is surrounded by fragments that she can't fully integrate into a cohesive whole. But *we* bring a further order to these fragments by gathering them *into a reading*: by telling a coherent story about *why* the collector can't fully integrate them. The lessons of this story are counterintuitive and even paradoxical, since they say, in effect, that a book's failure to display a singular way of being *is* its most singular way of being. Its unity lies precisely in its lack of unity. To be sure, the order that we impose through this insight is a different and weaker kind of order than the one collectors might initially expect. It is, so to speak, a higher-order order. But it's no less real for that.

"Unpacking My Library" begins with images of disorder. It asks us to imagine a collector reopening crates of books that have endured "two years of darkness," and to inspect piles of books that have not yet been "touched by the mild boredom of order."[57] But the individual volumes are not the point; "collecting rather than a collection"[58] is the point. And collecting, we learn in the essay's first paragraphs, is a self-consciously ontological activity in that it establishes "a relationship to objects which does not emphasize their functional, utilitarian value—that is, their usefulness."[59] A real collector doesn't care what her books can *do* for her—how they can advance her research or fetch high prices at auction, say. Her only concern is that the objects get "their due"⁶⁰ by being recognized as the unique beings they are. To collect is to renounce our interests in these objects and simply let them be. Paradoxically, though, letting the objects be is something the collector must accomplish by acting on them. She doesn't simply find objects existing as the unique things they are. She must *make* them into such things, *transform* their mode of being through the act of collecting. As we've seen, Benjamin likens this transformation to "the locking of individual items within a magic circle."⁶¹ He makes clear that the items locked within this circle are not just physical volumes but virtual contents as well. The collector transforms what she collects by imposing order on it, and this order gets imposed on private experiences and memories of reading no less than on paper books. Collecting, Benjamin says, is "a dam against the spring tide of memories which surges toward any collector as he contemplates his possessions. Every passion borders on the chaotic, but the collector's passion borders on the chaos of memories."⁶² Collecting is thus an attempt to bring order to oneself as well as to one's shelves.

But this attempt can never fully succeed. "Unpacking My Library" insists that collecting involves a "dialectical tension between the poles of disorder and order,"⁶³ and the collector never fully inhabits either pole. The problem isn't just that collections tend to burst through any boundaries placed on them, acquiring "prismatic fringes"⁶⁴ made up of photo albums, autograph collections and other not-quite-books. Nor is the problem that the collector's impulse is "childlike" and slightly ridiculous, an attempt to "accomplish the renewal of existence" akin to "the painting of objects, the cutting out of figures, the application of decals—the whole range of childlike modes of acquisition, from touching things to giving them names."⁶⁵ No, the real problem is that the collector's goal is at war with itself. She wishes to relate to the objects she collects purely as things that are, things unsullied by her interests and actions. But she tries to bring about this transformation in their being by acting on them—by remaking them into things that, paradoxically, she has had no hand in making. She wants to remove an object from its contexts and view it acontextually. But she tries to do so by relocating the object to a new context—her shelves, of course, but also a history of the object's "fate" in which its "most important fate" is "its encounter with [her]."⁶⁶ In short, the collector sets herself the impossible task of imposing an order without imposing one, of leaving things exactly as they are by turning them into something other than what they are. And Benjamin's gentle mockery of the collector—as when he calls a collection a "disorder to which habit has accommodated itself to such an extent that it can appear as order"⁶⁷—suggests that he knows this.

But the story does not end here. Granted, "Unpacking My Library" presents the collector as someone who tries and fails to take up a fully coherent stance toward the things she reads. But a *reading* of this text opens up another stance. It is the meta-stance occupied by us as readers of the text. In a sense, we readers of "Unpacking My Library" actually accomplish what Benjamin's collector fails to accomplish: we give a coherent, unified account of the kind of being displayed by the objects collected. We do this precisely by calling these objects ones that cry out to be ordered but that frustrate our attempts to order them. We do so when we view collecting as the movement of trying to gather the different ways of being displayed by the things we read. For in viewing collecting in this way, we actually do impose a kind of unity on their diverse ways of being: the unity that belongs to the different moments of a single movement. We, as detached onlookers, are able to say something that the collector (at least in so far as she "disappears" inside the "dwelling" of her books[68]) cannot: that there is something that unites all her collected fragments, and it is precisely the lack of something that unites them. But we're able to say this only because of the unique perspective we occupy—a perspective opened up by the act of reading. The collector can't do this on her own. But the reader, by collecting the collectors, can.

The interpretation I've sketched here is just one example of how the activity of reading can involve ontological reflection. No doubt different readers, responding to different texts, might engage in different sorts of reflections. But I hope it conveys some sense of how the act of reading, and the experiences of those who engage in it, can contribute something distinctive to ontology. Ontology proves to be another of the ways in which the common reader can, to quote Woolf, "create for himself, out of whatever odds and ends he may come by, some kind of whole."[69]

Chapter 7

THE FUTURE OF THE COMMON READER

A Digital Future?

The main claim of this book has been that reading is a philosophical activity. I've looked at several different ways in which reading provides an opportunity to work through philosophical questions: that is, fundamental questions about distinctively human capacities. In doing so, I've been guided by the reports of common readers themselves. I've taken my cues from their own accounts of how reading has helped them to think through what a self is, what our moral responsibilities are and how we relate to things. Because of this focus on common readers, I've paid special attention to the reports of well-known readers from the past—sometimes the quite distant past. To shed light on how reading lets us reflect on the nature of things, I turned to texts by Lucian of Samosata and George Orwell. To help make sense of the idea that reading is a social practice governed by moral responsibilities, I looked at Machiavelli. Even when discussing newer documents, I've tended to discuss them in language borrowed from earlier stages in the history of reading. In the last chapter, for instance, I used the word "book" as an umbrella term for all the things we read. This old-fashioned language might suggest that the practice of *reading* and the practice of reading *printed books* are one and the same.

But as everyone knows, reading is changing. We appear to be living through one of the most dramatic shifts in the history of reading: a shift in which electronic screens are replacing paper and ink as the main way of encountering texts.[1] It seems likely that this technological shift will lead to dramatic changes in the practice of reading, and thus in the experiences of common readers. The move to electronic texts is so new that we don't yet understand it very well, and it's unwise to make many assumptions about it. But the early evidence suggests that the experience of reading onscreen is quite different from that of reading paper and ink—sometimes in troubling ways. Some studies suggest that the brain processes electronic texts quite differently than texts printed on paper, with screens making it harder to form memories and to pay sustained attention to what we read.² It's not yet clear why this might be; it's not clear whether the apparent problems with onscreen reading result from something essential to electronic texts, or from the difficulties of asking readers raised on paper to shift to a new medium. It's certainly possible that the problems associated with reading onscreen stem from the limitations of current technologies, and that they'll vanish or lessen as e-texts improve. Nevertheless, it's clear that reading is changing, and that the consequences, whatever they turn out to be, will be far-reaching.

Given all of this, my focus on the reports on common readers from the past might seem outdated and of limited interest. Isn't it inevitable that, as onscreen reading becomes the norm, serious readers will have very different experiences than they used to? And what if these experiences will no longer involve working through philosophical questions? In short, isn't it possible that reading's days as a philosophical activity are numbered? Does the common reader have a future?

Changing Practices

Perhaps we should turn this question around. Why *wouldn't* the common reader have a future? Why would we think that the shift from paper to screens will make reading incapable of performing a philosophical function? It seems to me that we would think this only if we made certain assumptions about the kinds of changes that it's possible for reading to undergo. We'd think this only if we assumed that the shift from paper to screens has to be an all or nothing affair, with onscreen reading *either* entirely unlike what preceded it, *or* not significantly different from it at all. We'd have to assume that the only two possibilities for this shift are a complete rupture in the history of reading—perhaps one that leaves reading unable to perform its earlier philosophical function—or a superficial change that leaves the substance of reading untouched. This assumption actually does seem to be at work in many discussions of the future of reading, though it's rarely articulated explicitly. It was voiced in the 1990s by Michael Hart, the founder of Project Gutenberg, who described electronic texts as "a new medium, with no real relationship to paper, other than presenting the same material."³ Hart went on to claim that electronic reading is not just a completely new type of reading; it has so many advantages over reading on paper that it's bound to supplant the earlier medium. "I don't see," Hart says, "how paper can possibly compete once people find their own comfortable way to etexts, especially in schools."⁴ Plenty of recent commentators have agreed with Hart that reading's future will be utterly different from its past. Some, like Hart, are optimistic about this. Clay Shirky suggests that the future is bound to be paperless, because e-books offer such advantages that there's no way printed books can compete with them. Shirky grants that the move away from paper will incur some costs—for example, a glut of bad writing that will make it harder to sift out the good stuff.[5] But he thinks that the "compensating values" of onscreen reading, such as an "increasing freedom to participate in the public conversation" and an "increase of experimentation of form,"[6] are too great to resist. Other commentators are more pessimistic. Maryanne Wolf, whose view of electronic reading is by no means entirely negative, worries that screens will cause a faster and more superficial type of reading to become the norm. She wonders: "Will this next generation's capacity to find insights, pleasures, pains, and wisdom in oral and written language be dramatically altered […]? Will the present generation become so used to onscreen information that the range of attentional, inferential, and reflective capacities in the present reading brain will become less developed?"[7] Naomi Baron,[8] Ferris Jabr[9] and Andrew Piper[10] all voice similar worries. They point to studies suggesting that our ability to learn from and remember what we read is linked in complex ways to the process of physically navigating printed texts—a process that, at least for now, electronic texts can't replicate very well. "Reading," as Piper succinctly puts it, "isn't only a matter of our brains; it's something we do with our bodies."[11] This bodes poorly for a future dominated by reading on screens.

Then there are commentators who think that reading onscreen isn't that different from reading paper, and that a future in which it's widespread won't be significantly different from reading's past. Nicholas Carr has defended a view of this sort—which is somewhat surprising, given the gloomy assessment of the Internet age advanced in his 2010 book *The Shallows*. In a much-discussed essay for the *Wall Street Journal*, Carr argues that electronic books not only won't supplant paper ones; they're really "just another format—an even lighter-weight, more disposable paperback."[12] He points out that after a brief, early boom—one he attributes to "early adopters, a small but enthusiastic bunch"—sales of e-books have slowed, with "a whopping 59% of Americans" saying "that they have 'no interest' in buying one."[13] What's more, "nearly 90% of e-book readers continue to read physical volumes. The two forms seem to serve different purposes."[14] Screens are perfect for books that we skim quickly and then forget, or for those books, like *Fifty Shades of Grey*, that we don't want to be seen reading. But according to Carr, there's no risk of them becoming the main medium for reading, much less the only one. They are "a complement to traditional reading, not a substitute."[15]

Despite his disagreements with optimists like Shirky and pessimists like Wolf, Carr seems to share their assumption that the only options for reading's future are total change or no change at all. But this assumption is deeply at odds with the view of reading that I've defended in this book. I've repeatedly urged that we view reading as a practice, in MacIntyre's distinctive sense: a complex social activity that pursues internal goods and that, in the course of doing so, helps its practitioners achieve certain standards of excellence. As we've seen, one benefit of viewing reading as a practice is that it sheds light on aspects of reading that would otherwise be mysterious. For example, it provides a way of explaining the sense that common readers have that their reading is governed by moral responsibilities. As I argued in Chapter 5, the existence of such responsibilities is more plausible when we see them as responsibilities to a practice, responsibilities whose point is to sustain a large-scale, multi-generational enterprise and to help it to flourish. But another advantage of viewing reading as a practice is that it helps explain how reading can evolve in ways that fall between the extremes of total change and complete stasis. When a practice survives for a significant amount of time—and especially when it becomes big enough and old enough to become what MacIntyre calls a *tradition*—it typically mutates in all sorts of ways while remaining one and the same practice. Many of these changes concern the goods that the practice pursues. The participants in a practice might refine their understanding of what those goods are, going from a vague grasp of the point of the practice to a more definite one. They might decide that an earlier understanding of those goods was mistaken in certain respects. They might think that the earlier understanding has led the practice to a dead end, and replace it with a new one that is subtly or starkly different. They might even conclude that their predecessors didn't really understand the point of the practice at all: that what the earlier participants took to be the point of the practice was really something secondary, and that the practice's *really* essential features hadn't been noticed by anyone before themselves. When a practice is reinterpreted and redirected in these ways, it can appear to some of its members to be coming to an end, to be giving rise to an utterly different activity with an utterly different point. It sometimes takes the perspective of a later observer to recognize that what seemed at the time to be the end of the practice was really a new stage in its development. Practices can retain their identity even while undergoing dramatic change.

MacIntyre illustrates all of this with a discussion of the philosophical tradition to which he himself belongs. Recall that for MacIntyre, traditions aren't identical with practices, but are closely related to them. Roughly, a tradition is what a practice becomes when it attains a degree of self-consciousness: when it becomes sufficiently old and well-established for its participants to "become aware of it and of its direction and in self-aware fashion attempt to engage in its debates and to carry its enquiries forward."[16] Since a tradition is an attempt to carry forward certain inquiries in self-aware fashion, it can be described as a kind of argument—namely, "an argument extended through time in which certain fundamental agreements are defined and redefined."[17] Above all, it's an argument about the goods to be pursued by that tradition. As we've seen several times, one of the distinctive features of practices, and therefore of traditions, is that they aim at internal goods, goods that are not reducible to external goods such as wealth or honour. These internal goods are available only to those who have been inculcated into the norms of a practice, and their value may not be clear to those who have not been so inculcated. We see one version of this in MacIntyre's chess example. A child might start out thinking that the point of playing chess is to win candy. But as he's inculcated into the practice and internalizes its standards, he comes to appreciate that its true rewards are quite different than he first thought.

MacIntyre gives a more complex example of this phenomenon in his discussion of his own philosophical tradition. This is the tradition of moral inquiry that finds its clearest expression in the writings of Aristotle, and later, in the Christian Aristotelianism of Saint Thomas Aquinas.[18] According to MacIntyre, this tradition originated in post-Homeric Greece as an argument about the relation between two kinds of goods: "goods of excellence"[19] that can be achieved by respecting "the standards established within and for some specific form of systematic activity"[20]—goods such as moral and intellectual virtue—and "goods of effectiveness"[21] won by success in public competitions, "independently of any desire for excellence"[22]—goods such as wealth and honour. One of the most interesting features of this tradition, as MacIntyre describes it, is that while it began as an argument about the relation of goods of effectiveness to goods of excellence, it didn't remain one. As centuries passed, the conversation that defined the tradition was redirected, and those participating in the conversation came to see the tradition as having quite a different point than its founders did. For example, Aristotle suggested that the tension between the two fundamental kinds of goods could be resolved if they were both seen as components of the search for the highest good—the good of human existence as such. He further argued that the quest for the highest good was inseparable from the search for a form of social and political life that could sustain this quest. When the tradition's members took up this suggestion, they didn't see themselves as replacing an old tradition with a new and better one. They saw themselves as discovering something about what their tradition had been all along—even though its founders did not and perhaps could not see this. The conversation was redirected yet again in the thirteenth century, when Thomas Aquinas synthesized the Aristotelian tradition with the doctrines of Catholic Christianity. Now the tradition came to be seen as a quest for a supernatural end, a good attainable only with the assistance of divine grace. And once again, those who redirected the tradition saw themselves as discovering something that had been implicit in it all along—even though Aristotle himself did not and probably could not have recognized it.

The point is that a continuous line of development unifies this tradition, from its earliest stages in post-Homeric Greece to its most recent stages exemplified by contemporary Aristotelians such as MacIntyre. At many points along the way, the tradition has changed dramatically. Not only have its members advanced very different conclusions; they have held very different views about what the point of their tradition is. At each such shift, some members of the tradition presumably thought it was coming to an end. No doubt some of Aristotle's contemporaries thought that shifting the focus away from the two kinds of goods and toward the highest good marked the end of the tradition. And no doubt, centuries later, some who thought that Aristotle had discovered the tradition's true nature believed that bringing it into contact with Christianity would prove fatal to it. Despite all these twists and turns, however, the tradition is recognizably the same tradition. Each stage emerges from earlier ones in a way that makes sense. Thus the emergence of change, even quite radical change, doesn't necessarily spell the end of a tradition.

Finally, it's important to note that the changes that redirect a tradition can have many different causes. MacIntyre's history of Aristotelianism focuses on changes that result from conscious argumentation—people changing their minds about this or that issue, being influenced by new ideas and books, and so on.[23] But changes in a tradition aren't always be driven by changes in ideas and arguments. Material changes, and particularly technological changes, can also play a decisive role. Consider warfare. As MacIntyre notes,[24] the ancient Greeks considered warfare to be a practice similar in many ways to philosophy. Like philosophy, it was understood to be an organized activity devoted to the pursuit of certain internal goods. Like philosophy, it was seen as allowing those who engaged in it to develop certain virtues. But it seems clear that later developments in the technologies of warfare have changed this practice so dramatically that the internal goods made available by it have become very different, or perhaps even vanished. Warfare became a very different undertaking as swords and muskets gave way to tanks and, later, nuclear weapons. One could certainly narrate a history of warfare in which the decisive events are technological changes—even as the existence of warfare remains constant.

Changing the Questions

MacIntyre's discussion of practices and traditions focuses mainly on their pasts. It claims that if we wish to understand a tradition as it currently is, we must view it against the backdrop of the history that gave rise to it—a history that involves both considerable change and significant continuity. But what interests me most about this discussion is what it implies about the future of practices and traditions. As MacIntyre notes, it is "part of the nature of traditions that their adherents cannot know in advance, whatever their own convictions or pretensions might be, how and in what condition their tradition will emerge" from its experiences of change.[25] It's always possible that a practice will be redirected in ways that are difficult or impossible for its current practitioners to foresee. It's always possible that at some point in the future, features that now seem absolutely central to the practice will come to seem much less so. And it's always possible that it will reach that later, very different stage in its development without ever ceasing to be the practice that it is. Practices evolve gradually and steadily, with each new stage appearing as the rational outcome of the one that preceded it. No matter how much the latest stages differ from the earliest stages, there is a recognizable line of continuity linking them—the continuity of an extended argument, an extended historical conversation. This continuity is compatible with its members believing that some particular change—be it a shift in ideas or a new set of material conditions—spells the end of the tradition. What now looks like the end of a practice might well appear, from the perspective of later participants, to be a refining and redefining of its point. It may even look like the triumphant discovery of what the practice has been doing all along, even though earlier participants failed to notice this.

Why couldn't reading evolve along similar lines? Yes, the practice of reading seems to be changing dramatically as a result of the shift from paper to screens. Yes, it's hard for contemporary readers to imagine how some of the features they consider central to that practice will survive the shift. But to conclude that the common reader has no future, or that reading will soon cease to be a philosophical activity, would be far too hasty. It's much more plausible to suppose that the technological shifts currently transforming reading are like the shifts that have transformed Aristotelian moral inquiry: innovations that couldn't have been predicted but that, in retrospect, look like redirections of an earlier tradition rather than rejections of it. Aristotelian moral inquiry is a continuous conversation about the nature of human flourishing, even though it has entertained many different ideas about which sorts of goods are relevant to that flourishing. Surely it's possible that the goods made available by the practice will be transformed and reinterpreted to a similar degree without bringing the practice to an end. More specifically, it's possible that the philosophical insights offered to common readers—the opportunities to think through fundamental questions about selfhood, morality and things—will evolve as the technologies of reading do, without ceasing to be philosophical.

Of course, it's impossible to know what reading's philosophical side will look like a hundred years from now, or even twenty years from now. But it's interesting to speculate about which aspects of it are likely to change, and which are likely to stay the same. Consider the topic of selfhood. As we saw in Chapters 2 and 3, the practice of reading offers the opportunity to think through the nature of selfhood. This is closely connected with what Iser calls the wandering viewpoint that is forced on readers: the fact that, since texts are never given as complete objects, readers must piece together the things they read by actively navigating through them. As Piper points out, navigating one's way through a physical book is "something we do with our bodies."[26] Physical books might make available different sorts of reflections on selfhood than any screen could ever do, and from that perspective, the waning of physical books might foreshadow the end of certain kinds of reflections on selfhood. But whether we read on paper or screens, any text longer than a few lines must be encountered through a wandering viewpoint. Electronic novels are inhabited and navigated differently than printed ones. But they're still inhabited and navigated, which means that at least some of the opportunities they provide to reflect on the nature of selfhood will endure—even if they change in ways we can't currently envision.

We could speculate in a similar vein about the sorts of ethical reflection occasioned by reading. It seems likely that, as our understanding of the reading self changes, our understanding of moral agents will change along with it. An age in which onscreen reading is the norm might be one in which some of the kinds of ethical reflection that common readers have long engaged in change or disappear. But new kinds might also emerge. Here it's worth recalling a point explored in Chapter 5: that some of the moral responsibilities readers think they have look like responsibilities to the practice of reading, responsibilities they share with their community of fellow readers. As their understanding of how they're related to that community changes, their view of those responsibilities will probably change along with it. And since electronic reading can heighten our awareness of our ties to other readers—as when an e-reader lets us see which parts of a text others have highlighted or annotated—a future dominated by screens could be a future with fascinating new opportunities for moral reflection.

Finally, it's interesting to speculate about how the shift to e-reading might reshape readers' encounters with things. As we saw in Chapter 6, what makes these encounters possible is the fact that a book's content—*Madame Bovary*, say—isn't a particular object, and so is distinct from the item that gives us access to it—such as a particular physical copy of *Madame Bovary*. This difference lets us divorce the book's virtual content from its physical incarnation, and to encounter the latter purely as a thing. Traditionally, when common readers have been spurred to reflect on the thingly character of what they read, they've focused on the physicality of printed books. Presumably they'll have fewer opportunities to do so as onscreen reading becomes the norm. But whatever new forms reading takes, there will still be a distinction between the content we read and the object that brings it to us. The new objects will, presumably, have different meanings than physical books, so they'll spur different sorts of reflections about what things, considered simply as things, mean to us. But the new objects might spur different reflections about the meanings of things that are just as interesting as the earlier ones.[27] Here again, there's little reason to think that reading's status as a philosophical activity will simply end.

In short, in each of the three areas I've considered, electronic reading promises significant changes in reading's philosophical side. But it also promises considerable continuity with the past. Obviously, it's important not to be a Pollyanna here. Reading for pleasure and doing philosophy strike many as luxuries, and it would be foolish to think that they could never be undermined by new technologies. But it would be just as foolish to think that the shift to digital screens, in and of itself, must signal the end of reading as a philosophical practice. Nearly every age makes dramatic announcements about how its dominant technologies will change humanity into something utterly unprecedented. As Williams Powers has pointed out, "history is replete with moments when some astonishing new invention came along that suddenly made it easier for people to connect across space and time. And those earlier shifts were as exhilarating and confusing to those who lived through them as today's are to us."[28] Few things ring so hollow as yesterday's claim that finally, for the first time, we've built a new machine that makes everything different.

Changing Philosophy

In short, there is every reason to be cautiously optimistic about the future of the common reader. As dramatic as the shift from paper to screens promises to be, there is little reason to fear it will abolish those features of reading that make it philosophical. In fact, I suspect that the grounds for optimism are even greater. To bring the book to a close, I'd like to sketch a stronger claim: that the changes reading seems to be undergoing have the potential to *strengthen* its philosophical side—even to strengthen *philosophy*, full stop, in a way that might help sustain and enrich it. I realize that this is a bold suggestion about something very much in flux. My argument for it will have to be speculative and inconclusive. But there is still an argument to be made here, and if I'm right, plenty of reason for hope.

First, a reminder. Throughout this book, I've tried to remain as neutral as possible on the question of what philosophy is. In particular, I've tried not to take a stand on the question of whether it has anything like a fixed nature, such that some topics and not others are the genuinely philosophical ones. This reticence will continue here. I'll assume that there are familiar and uncontroversial examples of philosophy that we can all recognize—ethics and ontology, for instance—but I won't try to say anything substantive about what makes them examples of philosophy. So nothing I say here should be taken as an attempt to define philosophy or to say the last word about it. The only thing on which I'll continue to insist is that philosophy not be seen in narrowly professional terms—as something that goes on in seminar rooms and journal articles but nowhere else. It does go on there, to be sure, but it also takes place in a much wider range of spheres—anywhere, in fact, where there is persistent reflection on distinctively human capacities. In particular, it takes place in the activities of common readers, in so far as they reflect on who and what they are, how they should live, and what things mean to them.

My optimism about reading's future stems from this expansive view of philosophy. To the extent that reading is a philosophical practice, then a change in the conduct of reading *is* a change in the conduct of philosophy—namely, in those cases of philosophy found in the activities of common readers. In that sense, as reading changes, philosophy can't help but change along with it. And as we've seen, one of the ways a practice can change is by becoming convinced that its nature is different than was previously believed. After all, practices are extended arguments that can and do take all sorts of twists and turns. What initially looks like the end of a practice can come to look like the discovery that, all along, its members have been arguing about something different than they thought they were. It is precisely such a discovery, I've suggested, that is currently unfolding in the practice of reading. Before the shift to screens, it was possible to maintain that reading's distinctive goods were essentially tied to the physicality of paper books. Plenty of common readers speak as if they are. Orwell links his early love of the book world to the "sweet smell of decaying paper" and his later disillusionment with it to the "boring and even slightly sickening" experience of encountering printed books "in the mass, five or ten thousand at a time."[29] Benjamin also speaks as though the rewards available to collectors depend essentially on the physicality of books—and not just their smell or appearance, but their locations in space, their presence in "the smallest antique shop" or "the most remote stationery store."[30] "How many cities have revealed themselves to me," he asks, "in the marches I undertook in the pursuit of books!"[31] If we take such language at face value, we might worry that the shift to screens heralds the end of reading as Orwell and Benjamin understand it. But to the extent that common readers' "instinct to create […] some kind of whole"[32] endures through the shift to screens, it looks as though we've made an exciting discovery: that reading's philosophical significance has *never* depended essentially on the smell of paper, the spatiality of bookshops, or any other particular physical property. It has always been about something more, even if no one was in a position to discover this until now.

Furthermore—and this is the crucial point—by learning *that* lesson, we simultaneously learn another, more abstract one: that reading is the *kind of thing* that can go through dramatic and unforeseeable changes without ceasing to be what it is, and without ceasing to offer its distinctive goods. Indeed, it is the kind of thing that can emerge from such changes stronger than before, in the sense that it knows itself better and has a firmer grasp of what is and isn't central to it. Radical change, far from destroying the practice, is an opportunity for it to reach a heightened degree of self-consciousness. When we combine this insight with the awareness that reading is a philosophical practice, the implications are even more encouraging. For it follows that *philosophy* is also the kind of thing that can endure dramatic and seemingly threatening changes without ceasing to be what it is, emerging from these changes stronger than ever. In this sense, the shift to screens looks like an opportunity for philosophy to come to know itself better, to get a clearer sense of what has and hasn't been important to it all along. One of the lessons philosophy learns by doing so is that seminar rooms and journal articles have never been as central to it as one might suppose. Another, closely related lesson is that philosophy is more adaptable and more resilient than it sometimes appears.

Philosophy has probably always needed to be reminded of this. It has often found itself torn between broader and narrower images of itself. According to the broader image, it is a universalistic enterprise, a form of questioning to which everyone is instinctively drawn. According to the narrower image, it is something more rarified: a specialized and technical pursuit open only to those with advanced training. The tension between these images is personified in the Socrates of Plato's dialogues, who alternates between presenting his questions as universal ones that should occur to everyone, and addressing these questions through extraordinarily abstruse reflections on the one and the many, the limited and the unlimited, being and non-being. Philosophy has probably always needed to be reminded that these images don't exclude each other: that both capture something important, and that philosophy's different sides have the potential to strengthen and enhance one another. But such reminders seem particularly important today. In many contemporary universities, philosophy is a marginal discipline, garnering little respect and having even less influence. No doubt there are many reasons for this state of affairs, having to do with sweeping social and economic developments as well as large-scale trends in higher education. Some philosophers, however, blame the discipline itself,[33] and draw discouraging conclusions about its future.

Consider the case of Richard Rorty. He spent much of his career as a consummate academic insider, a long-time faculty member at Princeton and a president of the American Philosophical Association's Eastern Division. As he later recounted, Rorty was at first hopeful that the developments known as "the linguistic turn" had put philosophy on the path to genuine progress, perhaps even enabling it to solve its perennial problems and "hold reality and justice in a single vision."[34] He eventually came to see this hope as misguided, a young scholar's attempt "to persuade himself that the disciplinary matrix in which he happened to find himself (philosophy as taught in most English-speaking universities in the 60s) was more than just one more philosophical school, one more tempest in an academic teapot."[35] Rorty seems to have been disillusioned by the discovery that academic philosophy couldn't accomplish everything that his youthful self had sought—so disillusioned that his later work sometimes seems to give up on philosophy's traditional aspirations altogether. By the turn of the millennium, Rorty was calling philosophy a "transitional genre,"[36] a bridge from a culture dominated by religion to one dominated by literature. He claimed that it is now "literary culture,"[37] and especially the reading of novels, that allows people to reflect fruitfully on the questions that matter most to them. Philosophy as done in universities is no substitute for such reflection, and is best seen as a stage on the path to a mature literary culture—a "glorious" stage, perhaps, but a "relatively primitive" one.[38]

Rorty's late pessimism about philosophy flows, I think, from the assumption that it is nothing more and nothing less than what certain academics do in journal articles and seminar rooms. It is decidedly *not* what goes on in the experiences and reflections of common readers. If these experiences and reflections seem more relevant to most peoples' lives than the journals and seminars do, then the proper conclusion to draw is that *philosophy* has lost its relevance and been supplanted by literary culture. But from the perspective I've sketched in this book, matters look quite different. From this perspective, there is no antithesis between literary culture and philosophy, or between the reflections of common readers and the specialized scholarship that Rorty thinks has been superseded. Both deserve to be called philosophy. And if the specialized scholarship has become marginalized, it does not follow that philosophy as such has been marginalized. It might be thriving—merely in different forms and different sites than the ones we have come to expect. To be clear, I don't mean to denigrate seminar rooms or journal articles, or suggest that the experiences of common readers can replace them. Philosophy as a specialized scholarly activity is indispensable, and we should defend it, and strengthen it, as best we can. All I'm suggesting is that there might be unexpected benefits in recognizing reading as a philosophical practice. It might spur us to view philosophy as not simply besieged, not simply marginal, despite the challenges faced by university philosophy departments today. It might help us to notice how many different forms philosophy takes, and how lively some of the overlooked ones are.

    This is why I'm cautiously optimistic about the future of reading and the future of philosophy. Though the challenges that lie ahead are daunting, they may help these enterprises to come to know themselves better. And what could be more philosophical than that?

NOTES

Chapter 1 Philosophizing about Reading: The Very Idea

1. Mark Taylor, "The Impact of Reading on Career Prospects," *Books for Keeps* 189 (2011).
2. Maja Djikic et al., "On Being Moved by Art: How Reading Fiction Transforms the Self," *Creativity Research Journal* 21:1 (2009), 24–29.
3. Paulo Freire, "The Importance of the Act of Reading," *Journal of Education* 165:1 (1983), 11.
4. Cited in Christopher Ingraham, "Leisure Reading in the U.S. Is at an All-Time Low," *Washington Post* (29 June 2018), https://www.washingtonpost.com/news/wonk/wp/2018/06/29/leisure-reading-in-the-u-s-is-at-an-all-time-low (accessed 12 March 2020).
5. National Endowment for the Arts, *Reading on the Rise: A New Chapter in American Literacy*, 2009, http://nea.gov/research/ReadingonRise.pdf.
6. Danielle Fuller, "Citizen Reader: Canadian Literature, Mass Reading Events and the Promise of Belonging," in *The Fifth Eccles Centre for American Studies Plenary Lecture* (London: Eccles Centre and the British Library, 2011).
7. Pierre Bayard, *How to Talk about Books You Haven't Read*, trans. Jeffrey Mehlman (New York: Bloomsbury, 2007), xvi.
8. Alan Jacobs also makes this point. See Alan Jacobs, *The Pleasures of Reading in an Age of Distraction* (Oxford: Oxford University Press, 2011), 113.
9. Harold Bloom, *How to Read and Why* (New York: Touchstone, 2000), 19.
10. Mark Edmundson, *Why Read?* (New York: Bloomsbury, 2004), 4.
11. Jonathan Franzen, *How to Be Alone* (New York: Farrar, Straus and Giroux, 2002), 6.
12. Stephen Mulhall, *On Film*, 2nd ed. (London: Routledge, 2008), especially chapter 5.
13. Richard Rorty, "The Historiography of Philosophy: Four Genres," in *Philosophy in History*, ed. Richard Rorty, J. B. Schneewind and Quentin Skinner (Cambridge: Cambridge University Press, 1984), 58–59.
14. Jacobs, *The Pleasures of Reading in an Age of Distraction*, 107.
15. Bloom, *How to Read and Why*, 22.
16. Jacobs, *The Pleasures of Reading in an Age of Distraction*, 135.
17. Adia Mendelson-Maoz, "Ethics and Literature: Introduction," *Philosophia* 35 (2007), 111.
18. Walter Benjamin, "Unpacking My Library," in *Illuminations*, trans. Harry Zohn, ed. Hannah Arendt (New York: Shocken, 1968), 60.
19. Franzen, *How to Be Alone*, 6.
20. Ibid., 77.

21 Michael Benton, "Reading Fiction: Ten Paradoxes," *British Journal of Aesthetics* 22 (1982), 305.
22 Ibid., 305.
23 Roman Ingarden, *The Cognition of the Literary Work of Art*, trans. Ruth Ann Crowley and Kenneth R. Olson (Evanston, IL: Northwestern University Press, 1973), 13. Reading's active side is remarked upon much more often than its passive side. Some theorists go so far as to describe reading as simply active and not at all passive. Daniel Coleman, for example, claims that reading is "active *rather than* passive, being imaginative and dialogical." See Daniel Coleman, *In Bed with the Word: Reading, Spirituality, and Cultural Politics* (Edmonton: University of Alberta Press, 2009), 26, emphasis added. A few pages later, Coleman echoes this point when he says that "whereas the consumption of sensory-rich media is fast and passive, reading is slow and active. Readers must do the actual mental and physical labor of tracing the lines of print across the page, across page after page, and to exercise their capacities for recognition, comprehension, and imagination to create meaning from it" (30).
24 Benton, "Ten Paradoxes," 308.
25 Ibid., 308.
26 Andrew Piper, *Book Was There: Reading in Electronic Times* (Chicago: University of Chicago Press, 2012), x.
27 René Descartes, *Rules for the Direction of the Mind*, in *The Philosophical Writings of Descartes*, vol. 1, trans. and ed. John Cottingham, Robert Stoothoff and Dugald Murdoch (Cambridge: Cambridge University Press, 1985), 13.
28 John Russon, "Reading: Derrida in Hegel's Understanding," *Research in Phenomenology* 36 (2006), 181.
29 An important exception is Sarah Worth's recent book *In Defense of Reading* (London: Rowman and Littlefield, 2017). Like me, Worth is concerned with ordinary reading for pleasure, and like me, Worth thinks this sort of reading matters for philosophical reasons—that is, because it's connected to some of the central questions of philosophy. But there are also important differences in our approaches. As I read her, Worth thinks reading's philosophical importance is mostly ethical: "reading benefits us greatly" (xiii) in that it helps make us (morally) better people. My view, by contrast, is that reading is connected to *several* sorts of philosophical questions, including questions about selfhood and ontology—not just ethical questions. Another important difference is my belief that reading can't be fully understood unless it's viewed as a *practice*, in Alasdair MacIntyre's sense of the term. I have more to say about that point later in this chapter.
30 Bloom, *How to Read and Why*, 19.
31 Russon, "Reading: Derrida in Hegel's Understanding," 181.
32 Again, Worth is an important exception. She argues that although "philosophical questions about the effects of reading literature are well-trodden, […] philosophers have been too myopic about their arguments." See Worth, *In Defense of Reading*, xv.
33 Obviously this is a sweeping claim. When I say that deconstruction focuses less on reading than on the conditions that precede it, I have in mind the many texts in which Derrida characterizes *différance* as that which makes meaning possible at the same time that it destroys a certain ideal of meaning as pure presence. There are many such texts; one of the best known is the essay "Différance," which speaks of "the play which makes possible nominal effects, the relatively unitary and atomic structures that are

called names, the chains of substitutions of names in which, for example, the nominal effect *différance* is itself *enmeshed*." See Jacques Derrida, "Différance," in *Margins of Philosophy*, trans. Alan Bass (Chicago: University of Chicago Press, 1982), 26–27. Another well-known example is the discussion of "the book" in Jacques Derrida, *Dissemination*, trans. Barbara Johnson (Chicago: University of Chicago Press, 1981). As for hermeneutics, I have in mind the claim made by Gadamer (and echoed by many others) that the reading of a text is an event of understanding made possible by the prejudices that readers inherit from tradition. See especially Part II of Hans-Georg Gadamer, *Truth and Method*, 2nd ed., trans. Joel Weinsheimer and Donald Marshall (New York: Crossroad, 1992). Despite all this talk about the conditions that precede reading, I do not want to suggest that Derrida or Gadamer are transcendental philosophers in any straightforward or traditional sense. Both philosophers are known for putting transcendental inquiry in question—without rejecting it altogether. For a good summary of the way reading is approached by Derrida, Gadamer and related figures, see Thomas McCormick, *Theories of Reading in Dialogue: An Interdisciplinary Study* (Lanham, MD: University Press of America, 1988).
34 Plato's *Phaedrus* and Descartes's *Rules* seem to fall into this category.
35 Well-known examples are Martha Nussbaum, *Poetic Justice* (Boston, MA: Beacon Press, 1995) and Richard Rorty, *Contingency, Irony, and Solidarity* (Cambridge: Cambridge University Press, 1989).
36 See, for example, Susan Feagin, *Reading with Feeling* (Ithaca, NY: Cornell University Press, 1996).
37 I am not the first to use Woolf's essay as a model in a study of reading. Anne Fadiman, for one, has also done so. For several years, she wrote a column called "The Common Reader" for *Civilization*, and she published these columns as a book entitled *Ex Libris: Confessions of a Common Reader* (New York: Farrar, Strauss and Giroux, 1998).
38 Virginia Woolf, *The Common Reader: First Series*, ed. Andrew McNeillie (New York: Harcourt, 1984), 1.
39 Ibid.
40 Ibid.
41 Ibid.
42 Ibid.
43 Alasdair MacIntyre, *After Virtue*, 3rd ed. (Notre Dame, IN: University of Notre Dame Press, 2007), 187.
44 Bayard, *How to Talk about Books You Haven't Read*, xviii.

Chapter 2 The Reading Self

1 Fadiman, *Ex Libris*, ix.
2 Henry James, *Theory of Fiction*, ed. James Miller (Lincoln: University of Nebraska Press, 1972), 93.
3 Stanley Cavell, "The Avoidance of Love," in *Must We Mean What We Say?* (Cambridge: Cambridge University Press, 2002), 322.
4 Marcel Proust, "On Reading," in *Reading in Bed*, trans. Jean Autret and William Buford, ed. Steven Gilbar (Boston, MA: D. R. Godine: 1995), 41.
5 Chun-Ting Hsu, Markus Conrad and Arthur Jacobs, "Fiction Feelings in Harry Potter: Haemodynamic Response in the Mid-Cingulate Cortex Correlates with Immersive Reading," *Neuroreport* 25:17 (2014), 1356–61.

6 Ibid., 1356.
7 Jacobs, *The Pleasures of Reading in an Age of Distraction*, 30. To be fair, Jacobs goes on to say that this reaction is "largely unfair" to the scientists: "Of course they are talking about reading—just a different aspect of reading than I am habitually interested in" (30).
8 Of course, the *term* "phenomenology" did not originate with Husserl. It dates to at least the mid-eighteenth century.
9 See, for example, Ingarden, *The Cognition of the Literary Work of Art*, and Roman Ingarden, *The Literary Work of Art*, trans. George Grabowicz (Evanston, IL: Northwestern University Press, 1973).
10 Levinas is not usually thought of as someone who contributes to the phenomenology of reading. However, Colin Davis argues persuasively that something close to a phenomenology of reading appears in Levinas's essay "The Other in Proust." See Colin Davis, "Levinas and the Phenomenology of Reading," *Studia Phaenomenologica* 6 (2006), 275–92; and Emmaunel Levinas, "The Other in Proust," in *The Levinas Reader*, ed. Seán Hand (Oxford: Blackwell, 1989), 160–65.
11 Wolfgang Iser, *The Act of Reading: A Theory of Aesthetic Response*, trans. David Henry Wilson (Baltimore, MD: Johns Hopkins University Press, 1978), 19.
12 Ibid., 10.
13 Ibid., 18.
14 Wolfgang Iser, *The Implied Reader: Patterns of Communication in Prose Fiction from Bunyan to Beckett*, trans. David Henry Wilson (Baltimore, MD: Johns Hopkins University Press, 1974), xi.
15 Iser, *The Act of Reading*, 107.
16 Ibid., 38.
17 Ibid., 126.
18 Ibid., 140.
19 Ibid., 108–9.
20 Ibid., 109.
21 Ibid., 108.
22 Ibid., 109.
23 Ibid., 118.
24 Ibid., 124.
25 Ibid., 112.
26 Ibid., 109.
27 Ibid., 119.
28 Ibid., 126. He goes on to note that "in the early days of the novel, during the seventeenth century, such reading was regarded as a form of madness, because it meant becoming someone else" (156).
29 Ibid., 140.
30 A well-known popular treatment of this topic is Mihaly Csikszentmihalyi, *Flow: The Psychology of Optimal Experience* (New York: Harper Perennial, 2007).
31 For example, in the section of *Truth and Method* entitled "The Temporality of the Aesthetic," Gadamer characterizes play as the experience of "being totally involved in and carried away by what one sees." See Gadamer, *Truth and Method*, 125.
32 Iser, *The Act of Reading*, 140.
33 Ibid.
34 Ibid.

35   On the coming of evening, I return to my house and enter my study; and at the door I take off the day's clothing, covered with mud and dust, and put on garments regal and courtly; and reclothed appropriately, I enter the ancient courts of ancient men, where, received by them with affection, I feed on that food which only is mine and which I was born for, where I am not ashamed to speak with them and ask them the reason for their actions; and they in their kindness answer me; and for four hours of time I do not feel boredom, I forget every trouble, I do not dread poverty, I am not frightened by death; entirely I give myself over to them.

Niccolo Machiavelli, "Letter to Francesco Vettori, His Benefactor," in *The Prince*, trans. C. E. Detmold (London: Wordsworth, 1997), 128.

36   Fadiman, *Ex Libris*, 21.
37   George Orwell, "Bookshop Memories," in *An Age Like This: The Collected Essays, Journalism and Letters of George Orwell, Volume One*, ed. Sonia Orwell and Ian Angus (London: Secker and Warburg, 1968), 246.
38   Iser, *The Act of Reading*, 10.
39   Ibid., 119, emphasis added.
40   Franzen, *How to Be Alone*, 77.
41   Fadiman, *Ex Libris*, ix.
42   Woolf, *The Common Reader: First Series*, 1.
43   Wayne Booth echoes this point when he accuses Iser of being "chary of affective responses to the text," of refusing to "talk about the text arousing any desire except for our interest in its 'meaning,'" and of neglecting "matters like laughter, tears, fear, horror, disgust, joy, and celebration." See Wolfgang Iser, Norman Holland and Wayne Booth, "Interview: Wolfgang Iser," *Diacritics* 10:2 (Summer 1980), 67.
44   Ibid., 70.
45   Ibid.
46   Martin Heidegger, *Being and Time*, trans. John Macquarrie and Edward Robinson (San Francisco: Harper San Francisco, 1962), 86.
47   See Emmanuel Levinas, *Totality and Infinity*, trans. Alphonso Lingis (Pittsburgh: Duquesne University Press, 1969), especially 204–12.
48   Aaron Ridley, *Philosophy of Music: Theme and Variations* (Edinburgh: Edinburgh University Press, 2004), 1. Ridley uses this phrase to describe music, and elaborates on his point as follows:

In common with everything else, music occupies a conceptual space, not in a vacuum, but at the interstices of an indefinitely large and shifting set of other concerns, each of which it conditions and is conditioned by. Thus, through dance, music is tied reciprocally to sex and sociality; through hymns and chants to the health of the soul; through nursery rhymes to play; through marches to the army; through anthems to solidarity; through proportion to mathematics; through the *chantier* to work; through dirges to death; and so on. It is this embeddedness that gives music much of its richness, as well as accounting, through the fluctuating composition of its conceptual environment, for all its history. I am convinced that any attempt to understand music which tries to suppress this about it—the fact that it is embedded and historical—will be thin and unsatisfactory at best, and almost certainly worse than that. (2)

49   MacIntyre, *After Virtue*, 187.

Chapter 3 The Reading Life

1. Nick Hornby, *The Polysyllabic Spree* (San Francisco: Believer Books, 2004), 30.
2. Ibid., 13.
3. Bayard, *How to Talk about Books You Haven't Read*, 6.
4. Arthur Schopenhauer, "On Books and Writing," in *Essays and Aphorisms*, trans. R. J. Hollingdale (London: Penguin, 1970), 210.
5. Nick Hornby, *More Baths Less Talking* (San Francisco: Believer Books, 2012), 27.
6. Nick Hornby, *Shakespeare Wrote for Money* (San Francisco: Believer Books, 2008), 81.
7. Hornby, *The Polysyllabic Spree*, 90.
8. Hornby, *More Baths Less Talking*, 105.
9. Hornby, *The Polysyllabic Spree*, 13.
10. Ibid., 37.
11. Hornby's longest discussion of this topic appears in his preface to *Housekeeping vs. the Dirt*, the second collection of columns from Stuff I've Been Reading. *Housekeeping vs. the Dirt* was published in September 2006; the columns that it reprints originally appeared between February 2005 and July 2006.
12. Nick Hornby, *Housekeeping vs. the Dirt* (San Francisco: Believer Books, 2006), 14.
13. Ibid., 16.
14. Ibid., 17.
15. Hornby, *The Polysyllabic Spree*, 14.
16. Hornby, *Housekeeping vs. the Dirt*, 17.
17. Ibid., 18.
18. Ibid., 49.
19. Ibid., 57.
20. Ibid.
21. Ibid., 12.
22. William Hazlitt, "On Reading Old Books," in *Reading in Bed: Personal Essays on the Glories of Reading*, ed. Steven Gilbar (Boston, MA: D. R. Godine, 1995), 8.
23. Ibid.
24. Patricia Meyer Spacks, *On Rereading* (Cambridge, MA: Harvard University Press, 2011), 3.
25. Nabokov, *Lectures on Literature*, ed. Fredson Bowers (San Diego: Harvest, 1980), 3.
26. Spacks, *On Rereading*, 13.
27. Hornby, *The Polysyllabic Spree*, 77.
28. Hornby, *Shakespeare Wrote for Money*, 45.
29. Ibid.
30. Ibid.
31. Ibid., 75.
32. Ibid.
33. Ibid., 76.
34. For example, Spacks's *On Rereading* and Anne Fadiman's *Rereadings* (New York: Farrar, Strauss Giroux, 2006).
35. Hornby, *The Polysyllabic Spree*, 29.
36. Ibid., 53.
37. Hornby, *More Baths Less Talking*, 43. Hornby continues: "It never seems to occur to these critics that the deficiency may well lie within themselves, rather than in the pages of the books. Perhaps they feel similarly about their friends, parents, children. 'The

trouble with my kid is that she just doesn't make me *care* enough about her.' Are we all supposed to nod sagely at that?"
38 Hornby, *The Polysyllabic Spree*, 60.
39 Ibid., 104.
40 Ibid.
41 Hornby, *Shakespeare Wrote for Money*, 39.
42 He says, for example, that his very first month writing the column "was pretty much the last time my reading had any kind of logic or shape to it. Ever since then my choice of books has been haphazard, whimsical, and entirely shapeless" (Hornby, *Housekeeping vs. the Dirt*, 11).
43 Hornby, *The Polysyllabic Spree*, 13.
44 Michael Slote, *Goods and Virtues* (Oxford: Clarendon Press, 1983), 23–24.
45 John Martin Fischer, *Our Stories: Essays in Life, Death, and Free Will* (Oxford: Oxford University Press, 2009), 146.
46 MacIntyre, *After Virtue*, 219.

Chapter 4 Ethics *from* Reading?

1 Brad Stetka, "Why Everyone Should Read *Harry Potter*," *Scientific American* (9 September 2014), http://www.scientificamerican.com/article/why-everyone-should-read-harry-potter (accessed 12 July 2017).
2 Ibid.
3 For example, David Kidd and Emanuele Castano have found that the process of reading helps develop a reader's "theory of mind"—her understanding that others have thoughts and feelings. See David Kidd and Emanuele Castano, "Reading Literary Fiction Improves Theory of Mind," *Science* 342:6156 (18 October 2013), http://science.sciencemag.org/content/342/6156/377 (accessed 12 July 2017).
4 Wayne Booth, *The Company We Keep: An Ethics of Fiction* (Berkeley: University of California Press, 1988), 5.
5 See Rorty, *Contingency, Irony, and Solidarity*, especially chapters 7 and 8.
6 Andrew Gibson, *Postmodernity, Ethics and the Novel* (London: Routledge, 1999).
7 Colin McGinn, *Ethics, Evil and Literature* (Oxford: Clarendon Press, 1997).
8 Bloom, *How to Read and Why*, 22.
9 Hornby, *Shakespeare Wrote for Money*, 17.
10 Gregory Currie, "Does Great Literature Make Us Better?," *New York Times Opinionator* (1 June 2013), https://opinionator.blogs.nytimes.com/2013/06/01/does-great-literature-make-us-better (accessed 12 July 2017).
11 Currie has since explored these issues at greater length in his book *Imagining and Knowing: The Shape of Fiction* (Oxford: Oxford University Press, 2020). In that book, he again insists that only empirical evidence can answer the question of whether literature offers moral improvement. To those who suggest that "setting up literature to be judged by the standards of science [is] setting it up to fail" (7), he replies, "No. The standard of science is empirical evidence, and that is, or should be, everyone's standard—at least in factual matters" (8).
12 My response to Currie is therefore different from the one Sarah Worth gives in her book *In Defense of Reading*. Worth, as I understand her, accepts Currie's way of framing the debate about reading's possible moral benefits. She agrees that the important question is whether there is or isn't evidence that reading is morally beneficial (though

in the book's conclusion, she does express some reservations about the focus on evidence and measuring). She simply believes, against Currie, that "we do, in fact, have quite a bit of evidence that reading benefits us greatly" (xiii). I, on the other hand, resist this way of framing the issue on the grounds that before we can know *whether* reading benefits us, we must think more broadly about *how* it might do so.

13 To be fair, Currie acknowledges some of this. He grants that there are all sorts of ways in which reading *might* lead to moral improvement, and that it can be helpful to "have in mind a stock of ideas about ways literature might enhance our thought and action." But he doesn't endorse any of the ideas from his own personal stock; he doesn't single out any explanation as being more plausible, more worthy of empirical testing, than others. So his insistence that we seek "direct, causal evidence" of reading's moral benefits gets us only so far. How can we seek direct evidence of causal links without having some hunches about where to look?

14 I borrow this term from Simon Stow. See Simon Stow, "Reading Our Way to Democracy? Literature and Public Ethics," *Philosophy and Literature* 30:2 (2006), 413.

15 Nussbaum, *Poetic Justice*, xii.

16 Ibid., xv.

17 Ibid., 36.

18 Ibid.

19 Ibid., 38.

20 Ibid.

21 Ibid., emphasis added. It's unclear why we should assume, as Nussbaum apparently does, that the effects of fancy are always positive. Why should we think that reading literature leads us to interpret the actions of others in generous and charitable ways, rather than in ways that are neutral or even uncharitable? It's plausible to claim that reading trains us to look for deeper meanings, and to suspect that the actions of others have a significance that must be unearthed through interpretation. But why assume that this unearthing is always generous? Those trained to look for deeper meanings might do so generously on some occasions but ungenerously on others. They might even do so in consistently ungenerous ways. Someone who habitually reads novels with unreliable narrators, for example, might come to think that others are constantly trying to trick him, and thus to interpret their actions in ways that are ungenerous or even paranoid.

22 Ibid., 73.

23 Ibid., 72.

24 Ibid., 73.

25 Ibid.

26 Ibid.

27 Ibid., 90.

28 Ibid., 78.

29 Ibid., xv.

30 Ibid., 38, emphasis added.

31 Ibid., 78, emphasis added.

32 Ibid., 52.

33 Ibid., 96.

34 Stow, "Reading Our Way," 414.

35 Ibid.

36 Ibid., 413. To be fair, some of Nussbaum's work gives a more nuanced account of the reader's role in this process. *Love's Knowledge*, for example, explicitly addresses the contributions of readers, claiming that

> it is not ordinary readers, but theorists, who have sometimes felt that the pressure of a practical question would, rather like a sweaty hand on an exquisite leather binding, sully the text's purity of finish. Our actual relation to the books we love is already messy, complex, erotic. We do "read for life," bringing to the literary texts we love (as to texts admittedly philosophical) our pressing questions and perplexities, searching for images of what we might do and be, and holding these up against the images we derive from our knowledge of other conceptions, literary, philosophical, and religious.

See Martha Nussbaum, *Love's Knowledge* (Oxford: Oxford University Press, 1990), 29. Such talk of "searching" and "holding up" suggests that readers play a more active role in deriving ethical lessons from literature than Nussbaum suggests in *Poetic Justice*. That said, even in *Love's Knowledge*, Nussbaum's remarks about literature's ethical resources tend to privilege works over readers, and to suggest that works transmit their lessons to readers in a fairly straightforward way. One paragraph after the passage just quoted, for example, Nussbaum complains that those who seek philosophical instruction in literary works risk "ignoring in the process their *formal features* and their mysterious, various, and complex *content*" (29, emphasis added).

37 Gadamer, *Truth and Method*, 299, emphasis added.
38 Ibid., 300.
39 Hans-Georg Gadamer, *Reason in the Age of Science*, trans. Frederick Lawrence (Cambridge: MIT Press, 1981), 105.
40 Jay Parini, "The Considerable Satisfaction of Two Pages a Day," *Chronicle of Higher Education* (8 April 2005).
41 Stow, "Reading Our Way," 417. Stow explores this idea further in chapter 6 of his book *Republic of Readers? The Literary Turn in Political Thought and Analysis* (Albany: SUNY Press, 2008).
42 Stow, "Reading Our Way," 417.
43 Ibid.
44 Ibid., 418. Just as it's unclear why Nussbaum thinks the effects of fancy are generally positive, it's unclear why Stow thinks people discuss topics in a more considered way when these topics arise in discussions about literature. They might; they might be less passionate and more detached than they would be if they were seen to be discussing their own interests directly. But it seems just as likely that they will discuss these topics in a *less* considered way. Since they are not seen to be talking about themselves, they may feel less answerable for what they say, and thus freer to defend irresponsible positions recklessly.
45 Ibid., 417.
46 Ibid.
47 Quoted in Charles Reagan, *Paul Ricoeur: His Life and Work* (Chicago: University of Chicago Press, 1996), 108.
48 Paul Ricoeur, *Time and Narrative*, Volume Three, trans. Kathleen McLaughlin and David Pellauer (Chicago: University of Chicago Press, 1988), 101.
49 In *Truth and Method*, Gadamer puts the point this way: "Application does not mean first understanding a given universal in itself and then afterward applying it to a concrete

case. It is the very understanding of the universal—the text—itself. Understanding proves to be a kind of effect and knows itself as such." See Gadamer, *Truth and Method*, 341.
50 Heidegger, *Being and Time*, 93.
51 Indeed, Ricoeur explicitly links his use of the term "world" to Husserl's and Heidegger's. In his essay "The Hermeneutical Function of Distanciation," he says that narratives refer via "a second-order reference, which reaches the world not only at the level of manipulable objects but at the level that Husserl designated by the expression *Lebenswelt* and Heidegger by the expression *being-in-the-world*." See Paul Ricoeur, "The Hermeneutical Function of Distanciation," in *From Text to Action*, trans. Kathleen Blamey and John Thompson (Evanston, IL: Northwestern University Press, 1991), 85–86.
52 Paul Ricoeur, "The Model of the Text," in *From Text to Action*, 149.
53 Ricoeur, "The Hermeneutical Function of Distanciation," 86.
54 Paul Ricoeur, "Hermeneutics and the Critique of Ideology," in *From Text to Action*, 301. Gerald Bruns calls Ricoeur's view a "magical looking glass theory of textual meaning," since for Ricoeur,

> texts *mean* not by corresponding to states of affairs, not by satisfying truth conditions, but by manifesting or opening up a region of existence whose reality is not simply matter for analysis but is, on the contrary, matter for appropriation, for intervention and action. The task of discourse [is] not merely to picture reality but to throw light on the situation in which we find ourselves historically and open up a path for us to follow in the way of action and conduct.

See Gerald Bruns, *Hermeneutics, Ancient and Modern* (New Haven, CT: Yale University Press, 1992), 238.
55 Paul Ricoeur, *Oneself as Another*, trans. Kathleen Blamey (Chicago: University of Chicago Press, 1991), 164.
56 Bruns, *Hermeneutics, Ancient and Modern*, 238.
57 See Paul Ricoeur, *Time and Narrative*, Volume One, trans. Kathleen McLaughlin and David Pellauer (Chicago: University of Chicago Press, 1984), chapter 3.
58 See, among many other works, Amartya Sen, *Commodities and Capabilities* (Amsterdam: North Holland, 1985), and Martha Nussbaum, *Creating Capabilities: The Human Development Approach* (Cambridge, MA: Harvard University Press, 2011).
59 Nussbaum, *Creating Capabilities*, 35.

Chapter 5 Ethics *of* Reading?

1 The phrase "ethics of reading" is John Hillis Miller's. See John Hillis Miller, *The Ethics of Reading: Kant, de Man, Eliot, Trollope, James, and Benjamin* (New York: Columbia University Press, 1987).
2 In this chapter, I use the terms "ethical" and "moral" interchangeably. Not everyone does; in some contexts, the two are distinguished quite sharply. For a detailed discussion of this matter, see Robert Piercey, "Not Choosing between Morality and Ethics," *Philosophical Forum* 32:1 (March 2001), 53–72.
3 Mortimer J. Adler, *How to Read a Book* (New York: Touchstone, 1972), 138.
4 Ibid., 138–39, emphasis added.
5 Jacobs, *The Pleasures of Reading in an Age of Distraction*, 11.

6   Ibid., 15.
7   Ibid., 38.
8   Ibid., 41, emphasis added.
9   MacIntyre, *After Virtue*, 187.
10 Virgina Woolf, "How Should One Read a Book?," in *The Second Common Reader* (New York: Harcourt, 1932), 259.
11 Ibid., 266.
12 Ibid., 270.
13 Ibid., 267–68.
14 Ibid., 269.
15 Roger Crisp, "Deontological Ethics," in *The Oxford Companion to Philosophy*, ed. Ted Honderich (Oxford: Oxford University Press, 1995), 187–88.
16 Fadiman, *Ex Libris*, 37.
17 Georges Poulet, "Criticism and the Experience of Interiority," in *Reader Response Criticism: From Formalism to Post-Structuralism*, ed. Jane Tompkins (Baltimore, MD: Johns Hopkins University Press, 1980), 42.
18 Nussbaum, *Love's Knowledge*, 240.
19 Ibid.
20 Wayne Booth, *The Rhetoric of Fiction*, 2nd ed. (Chicago: University of Chicago Press, 1983), 73.
21 I am grateful to Candace Opper for suggesting this term.
22 Levinas, *Totality and Infinity*, 199.
23 Ibid., 42.
24 Wolfgang Iser, "The Reading Process: A Phenomenological Approach," in *Reader Response Criticism: From Formalism to Post-Structuralism*, 67.
25 Colin Davis, *Ethical Issues in Twentieth Century French Fiction: Killing the Other* (London: Macmillan, 2000), 1.
26 Ibid.
27 Ibid. emphasis added.
28 Richard Rorty, Jerome Schneewind and Quentin Skinner, "Introduction," in *Philosophy in History*, ed. Richard Rorty, Jerome Schneewind and Quentin Skinner (Cambridge: Cambridge University Press, 1984), 11.
29 MacIntyre, *After Virtue*, 187.
30 Ibid., 188.
31 Jacobs, *The Pleasures of Reading in an Age of Distraction*, 114.
32 Ibid., 115.
33 Woolf, *The Common Reader: First Series*, 1.
34 Franzen, *How to Be Alone*, 6.
35 Machiavelli, "Letter to Francesco Vettori," 109.
36 Alasdair MacIntyre, *Whose Justice? Which Rationality?* (Notre Dame, IN: University of Notre Dame Press, 1988), 327.

Chapter 6 Reading Things

1   For the rest of this chapter, I'll use the term "book" as shorthand for all the things we read, including plenty of things we normally distinguish from books: magazines, websites and so on. This expansive use of the term is not without problems, but there

is some precedent for it. Jacques Derrida, for instance, uses the term "book" in an exceedingly expansive way throughout his work.

2. For helpful discussions of this development and its significance, see Paul Saenger, *Space between Words: The Origins of Silent Reading* (Stanford, CA: Stanford University Press, 2000), and Jesper Svenbro, "Archaic and Classical Greece: The Invention of Silent Reading," in *A History of Reading in the* West, ed. Guglielmo Cavallo and Roger Chartier, trans. Lydia Cochrane (Amherst: University of Massachusetts Press, 1999), 37–63.

3. Alan Jacobs also makes this point. See *The Pleasures of Reading in an Age of Distraction*, 58.

4. Georges Poulet, "Criticism and the Experience of Interiority," in *Reader Response Criticism: From Formalism to Post-Structuralism*, 42. My distinction between virtual contents and physical tokens is much like Walter Benjamin's distinction between "books" and "copies of books." See Benjamin, "Unpacking My Library," 61.

5. Gabriel Marcel, *The Mystery of Being, Volume 1: Reflection and Mystery*, trans. G. S. Fraser (London: Harvill Press, 1951).

6. I have in mind here section 15 of *Being and Time*, where Heidegger distinguishes two major "categories" in terms of which things are understood: the "readiness to hand" of equipment and the "presence at hand" of objects we do not merely use. See *Being and Time*, 95–102. Also relevant here are texts such as "The Origin of the Work of Art," which argue that artworks should be seen as yet another sort of thing, a sort of thing not to be understood in terms of either readiness to hand or presence at hand. See Martin Heidegger, "The Origin of the Work of Art," in *Off the Beaten Track*, ed. and trans. Julian Young and Kenneth Haynes (Cambridge: Cambridge University Press, 2002), 1–56.

7. Benjamin, "Unpacking My Library," 60.

8. Ibid., 59.

9. The comparison with china appears in "Unpacking My Library" (62), where Benjamin attributes it to Anatole France.

10. Ibid., 60.

11. Ibid.

12. Ibid., 67.

13. Ibid.

14. Orwell, "Bookshop Memories," 246.

15. Ibid.

16. Ibid.

17. Jean-Paul Sartre, *Nausea*, trans. Lloyd Alexander (New York: New Directions, 1964), 127.

18. Baudrillard says that the objects people collect "are in fact the objects of a passion, that of personal possession," and that "what is characteristic of this passion is that it is tempered, diffuse, and regulative: we can only guess at its fundamental role in keeping the lives of the individual subject or of the collectivity on an even footing, and in supporting our very project of survival." See Jean Baudrillard, "The System of Collecting," in *The Cultures of Collecting*, trans. Roger Cardinal, ed. John Elsner and Roger Cardinal (Cambridge, MA: Harvard University Press, 1994), 7.

19. Lucian of Samosata, "Remarks Addressed to an Illiterate Book Fancier," trans. H. W. and F. G. Fowler, http://lucianofsamosata.info/RemarksOfIlliterateBookFancier.html#sthash.rdCnDgi0.dpbs (accessed 12 July 2017).

20. Quoted in Nicholas Basbanes, *Among the Gently Mad: Strategies and Perspectives for the Book Hunter in the 21st Century* (New York: Henry Holt, 2002), 1.

21 Adler, *How to Read a Book*, 49.
22 Quoted in Nicholas Basbanes, *A Gentle Madness: Bibliophiles, Bibliomanes, and the Eternal Passion for Books* (New York: Henry Holt, 1995).
23 Ibid., 277.
24 Joe Queenan, *One for the Books* (New York: Viking, 2012), 212.
25 Ibid.
26 Blumberg's story is told by Philip Weiss in "The Book Thief: A True Tale of Bibliomania." *Harper's Magazine*, 288:1724 (January 1994), 37–56. John Gilkey's story is told by Allison Hoover Bartlett in *The Man Who Loved Books Too Much: The True Story of a Thief, a Detective, and a World of Literary Obsession* (New York: Penguin, 2009).
27 That said, neither thief succeeds in relating to their books *purely* as objects. A recurring theme of both of their stories is that no matter how hard they try to see their books simply as objects to be collected, instrumental considerations always motivate them to some degree. Gilkey, for example, amasses an enormous collection that he doesn't use and can't show to anyone, but still takes pride in what owning all these books says about him. Bartlett reports that "it wasn't merely a love of books that compelled him, but also what owning them would say about him. It's a normal ambition—that our choice of music or cars or shoes reflects well on us—taken to the extreme" (Bartlett, *The Man Who Loved Books Too Much*, 47).
28 Peter Kivy, *The Performance of Reading: An Essay in the Philosophy of Literature* (Oxford: Blackwell, 2006), 5.
29 Robertson Davies describes one such reader, whom he calls "the most over-read girl I have ever known." Davies writes: "I can recall from my undergraduate days a girl who used to moan, when she was slightly drunk: 'I've read everything on the Senior English course lists, and where has it got me?' What she meant was that her reading had not provided her with beauty, or charm, or sexual irresistibility." See Robertson Davies, "Reading," in *The Merry Heart: Selections 1980–1995* (Toronto: McClelland and Stewart, 1996), 217. Strangely enough, Davies doesn't recall any male undergraduates whose reading was tainted by their desire for beauty, charm or sexual irresistibility.
30 Pamela Paul, "My Life with Bob," *New York Times* (13 April 2012).
31 Ibid.
32 Jacobs, *The Pleasures of Reading in an Age of Distraction*, 16.
33 Orwell, "Bookshop Memories," 242.
34 Roy MacSkimming, *The Perilous Trade: Publishing Canada's Writers* (Toronto: McLelland and Stewart, 2003), 360.
35 Bayard, *How to Talk about Books You Haven't Read*, xvi.
36 Ibid., 10.
37 Ibid., 40.
38 Ibid., 86.
39 Ibid., 45.
40 Ibid.
41 Ibid., 82–83.
42 Ibid., 83.
43 Ibid., 160n11.
44 Ibid., 160n11.
45 Ibid., 10–11.
46 Ibid., 40.
47 Ibid., 55.

48 For an entertaining discussion of this experience, see Patrick Süskind, "Amnesia in Litteris: The Books I Have Read (I Think)." *Harper's Magazine* (March 1987), 71–73.
49 Bayard, *How to Talk about Books You Haven't Read*, 129.
50 Ibid., 161.
51 Jay McInerney, "Faking It." *New York Times* (11 November 2007).
52 Bayard's core claim is that "we must consider just what is meant by *reading*, a term that can refer to a variety of practices" (xviii). Over the course of the book, Bayard suggests that this term is so obscure that the only real sense we can attach to it concerns being in touch with certain socially shared meanings. The clearest example of such contact is the practice of talking about a book with others. To talk about a book, in Bayard's revisionist sense, *is* to have read it. In Bayard's terms, therefore, talking about a book one hasn't read is a contradiction in terms. Critics who accuse him of advising us to talk about books we haven't read must not have read his book—which is, perhaps, entirely fitting.
53 Thomas Nagel, *The View from Nowhere* (Oxford: Oxford University Press, 1986), 3.
54 Ibid.
55 Robert Pippin, *After the Beautiful: Hegel and the Philosophy of Pictorial Modernism* (Chicago: University of Chicago Press, 2014), 141.
56 Heidegger, "The Origin of the Work of Art," 38.
57 Benjamin, "Unpacking My Library," 59.
58 Ibid., 60.
59 Ibid.
60 Ibid., 67.
61 Ibid., 60.
62 Ibid.
63 Ibid.
64 Ibid., 66.
65 Ibid., 61.
66 Ibid.
67 Ibid.
68 Ibid., 67.
69 Woolf, *The Common Reader: First Series*, 1.

Chapter 7 The Future of the Common Reader

1 Of course, not everyone agrees that screens will ever become the main medium through which people read. See, for example, chapter 5 of David Sax, *The Revenge of Analog: Real Things and Why They Matter* (New York, Public Affairs, 2016).
2 For a summary of this research, see Ferris Jabr, "Why the Brain Prefers Paper," *Scientific American* 309:5 (November 2013), 48–53.
3 Quoted in Lydia Pyne, *Bookshelf* (London: Bloomsbury, 2016), 23.
4 Ibid.
5 Clay Shirky, *Cognitive Surplus: How Technology Makes Consumers into Collaborators* (London: Penguin, 2010), 47.
6 Ibid.
7 Maryanne Wolf, *Proust and the Squid: The Story and Science of the Reading Brain* (New York: HarperCollins, 2007), 214.

8 Naomi Baron, *Words Onscreen: The Fate of Reading in a Digital World* (Oxford: Oxford University Press, 2015).
9 Jabr, "Why the Brain Prefers Paper." Jabr points to studies suggesting that the brain regards letters "as physical objects" and perceives "a text in its entirety as a kind of physical landscape" (48). The implications for e-reading are obviously worrisome, since—at least given current technology—"paper books have more obvious topography than on-screen text" (48).
10 Piper, *Book Was There*, 151–57.
11 Andrew Piper, "Out of Touch: E-Reading Isn't Reading," *Slate* (15 November 2012), https://slate.com/culture/2012/11/out-of-touch.html (accessed 2 October 2020).
12 Nicholas Carr, "Don't Burn Your Books—Print Is Here to Stay." *Wall Street Journal* (5 January 2013).
13 Ibid.
14 Ibid.
15 Ibid.
16 MacIntyre, *Whose Justice*, 327.
17 Ibid., 12.
18 For a fuller discussion of MacIntyre's view of this tradition, see my *The Uses of the Past from Heidegger to Rorty*, 102–6.
19 MacIntyre, *Whose Justice*, 32.
20 Ibid., 30.
21 Ibid.
22 Ibid., 32.
23 MacIntyre would probably object to this distinction between ideas and the material conditions in which they are embedded. In *A Short History of Ethics*, for example, MacIntyre denies that "there is merely an external, contingent causal relationship" between ideas and the forms of life that embody them. Instead, he argues that ideas are "partially constitutive" of forms of life. See Alasdair MacIntyre, *A Short History of Ethics*, 2nd ed. (Notre Dame, IN: University of Notre Dame Press, 1998), 1.
24 MacIntyre, *Whose Justice*, 30.
25 Ibid., 327.
26 Piper, "Out of Touch: E-Reading Isn't Reading."
27 An encouraging sign is that philosophers are starting to do interesting new research on the ontology of digital entities. See, for example, Yuk Hui, *On the Existence of Digital Objects* (Minneapolis: University of Minnesota Press, 2016). An especially valuable part of Hui's discussion is his insistence that digital objects (such as e-texts), though not physical, are still *particular* objects, even though they involve "new forms of both individuation and disindividuation" (xi).
28 William Powers, *Hamlet's Blackberry: A Practical Philosophy for Building a Good Life in the Digital Age* (New York: HarperCollins, 2010), 78.
29 Orwell, "Bookshop Memories," 246.
30 Benjamin, "Unpacking My Library," 63.
31 Ibid., 63.
32 Woolf, *The Common Reader: First Series*, 1.
33 A particularly clear expression of such a view is Robert Frodeman and Adam Briggle, *Socrates Tenured: The Institutions of 21st-Century Philosophy* (Lanham, MD: Rowman and Littlefield, 2016).

34 Richard Rorty, "Trotsky and the Wild Orchids," in *The Rorty Reader*, ed. Christopher Voparil and Richard Bernstein (Oxford: Wiley-Blackwell, 2010), 503.
35 Richard Rorty, "Twenty-Five Years After," in *The Rorty Reader*, 175.
36 Richard Rorty, "Philosophy as a Transitional Genre," in *The Rorty Reader*, 473.
37 Ibid., 476.
38 Ibid., 480.

BIBLIOGRAPHY

Baron, Naomi. *Words Onscreen: The Fate of Reading in a Digital World*. Oxford: Oxford University Press, 2015.
Bartlett, Allison Hoover. *The Man Who Loved Books Too Much: The True Story of a Thief, a Detective, and a World of Literary Obsession*. New York: Penguin, 2009.
Basbanes, Nicholas. *Among the Gently Mad: Strategies and Perspectives for the Book Hunter in the 21st Century*. New York: Henry Holt, 2002.
———. *A Gentle Madness: Bibliophiles, Bibliomanes, and the Eternal Passion for Books*. New York: Henry Holt, 1995.
———. *Patience and Fortitude*. New York: HarperCollins, 2001.
———. *A Splendor of Letters*. New York: HarperCollins, 2003.
Baudrillard, Jean. "The System of Collecting." In *The Cultures of Collecting*, trans. Roger Cardinal, ed. John Elsner and Roger Cardinal. Cambridge, MA: Harvard University Press, 1994, 7–24.
Bayard, Pierre. *How to Talk about Books You Haven't Read*, trans. Jeffrey Mehlman. New York: Bloomsbury, 2007.
Benjamin, Walter. "Unpacking My Library." In *Illuminations*, trans. Harry Zohn, ed. Hannah Arendt. New York: Shocken, 1968.
Benton, Michael. "Reading Fiction: Ten Paradoxes." *British Journal of Aesthetics* 22 (1982): 301–10.
Bloom, Harold. *How to Read and Why*. New York: Touchstone, 2000.
Booth, Wayne. *The Company We Keep: An Ethics of Fiction*. Berkeley: University of California Press, 1988.
———. *The Rhetoric of Fiction*, 2nd ed. Chicago: University of Chicago Press, 1983.
de Botton, Alain. *How Proust Can Change Your Life*. New York: Vintage, 1998.
Bruns, Gerald. *Hermeneutics Ancient and Modern*. New Haven, CT: Yale University Press, 1992.
Carr, Nicholas. "Don't Burn Your Books—Print Is Here to Stay." *Wall Street Journal*, 5 January 2013.
Cavell, Stanley. "The Avoidance of Love." In *Must We Mean What We Say?* Cambridge: Cambridge University Press, 2002, 267–353.
Coleman, Daniel. *In Bed with the Word: Reading, Spirituality, and Cultural Politics*. Edmonton: University of Alberta Press, 2009.
Crisp, Roger. "Deontological Ethics." In *The Oxford Companion to Philosophy*, ed. Ted Honderich. Oxford: Oxford University Press, 1995, 187–88.
Csikszentmihalyi, Mihaly. *Flow: The Psychology of Optimal Experience*. New York: Harper Perennial, 2007.

Currie, Gregory. "Does Great Literature Make Us Better?" *New York Times Opinionator* (1 June 2013). https://opinionator.blogs.nytimes.com/2013/06/01/does-great-literature-make-us-better. Accessed 12 July 2017.

———. *Imagining and Knowing: The Shape of Fiction*. Oxford: Oxford University Press, 2020.

Davies, Robertson. "Reading." In *The Merry Heart: Selections 1980–1995*. Toronto: McClelland and Stewart, 1996.

Davis, Colin. *Ethical Issues in Twentieth Century French Fiction: Killing the Other*. London: Macmillan, 2000.

———. "Levinas and the Phenomenology of Reading." *Studia Phaenomenologica* 6 (2006): 275–92.

Dehaene, Stanislas. *Reading in the Brain: The Science and Evolution of a Human Invention*. New York: Viking, 2009.

Derrida, Jacques. "Différance," In *Margins of Philosophy*, trans. Alan Bass. Chicago: University of Chicago Press, 1982, 26–27.

———. *Dissemination*, trans. Barbara Johnson. Chicago: University of Chicago Press, 1981.

Descartes, René. *Rules for the Direction of the Mind*. In *The Philosophical Writings of Descartes*, Volume 1, trans. and ed. John Cottingham, Robert Stoothoff and Dugald Murdoch. Cambridge: Cambridge University Press, 1985, 7–78.

Djikic, Maja, et al. "On Being Moved by Art: How Reading Fiction Transforms the Self." *Creativity Research Journal* 21:1 (2009): 24–29.

Edmundson, Mark. *Why Read?* New York: Bloomsbury, 2004.

Fadiman, Anne. *Ex Libris: Confessions of a Common Reader*. New York: Farrar, Strauss and Giroux, 1998.

———. *Rereadings*. New York: Farrar Strauss Giroux, 2006.

Feagin, Susan. *Reading with Feeling*. Ithaca, NY: Cornell University Press, 1996.

Fischer, John Martin Fischer. *Our Stories: Essays in Life, Death, and Free Will*. Oxford: Oxford University Press, 2009.

Foster, Thomas. *How to Read Literature Like a Professor*. New York: Harper Perennial, 2003.

Franzen, Jonathan. *How to Be Alone*. New York: Farrar, Straus and Giroux, 2002.

Freire, Paulo. "The Importance of the Act of Reading." *Journal of Education* 165:1 (1983): 5–11.

Frodeman, Robert, and Briggle, Adam. *Socrates Tenured: The Institutions of 21st-Century Philosophy*. Lanham, MD: Rowman and Littlefield, 2016.

Fuller, Danielle. "Citizen Reader: Canadian Literature, Mass Reading Events and the Promise of Belonging." *The Fifth Eccles Centre for American Studies Plenary Lecture*. London: Eccles Centre and the British Library, 2011.

Gadamer, Hans-Georg. *Reason in the Age of Science*, trans. Frederick Lawrence. Cambridge, MA: MIT Press, 1981.

———. *Truth and Method*, 2nd ed., trans. Joel Weinsheimer and Donald Marshall. New York: Crossroad, 1992.

Gibson, Andrew. *Postmodernity, Ethics and the Novel*. London: Routledge, 1999.

Hawes, James. *Why You Should Read Kafka before You Waste Your Life*. New York: St. Martin's, Press, 2008.

Hazlitt, William. "On Reading Old Books." In *Reading in Bed: Personal Essays on the Glories of Reading*, ed. Steven Gilbar. Boston, MA: D. R. Godine, 1995, 7–10.

Heidegger, Martin. *Being and Time*, trans. John Macquarrie and Edward Robinson. San Francisco: Harper San Francisco, 1962.

———. "The Origin of the Work of Art." In *Pathmarks*, ed. and trans. Julian Young and Kenneth Haynes. Cambridge: Cambridge University Press, 2002, 1–56.
Hornby, Nick. *Housekeeping vs. the Dirt*. San Francisco: Believer Books, 2006.
———. *More Baths Less Talking*. San Francisco: Believer Books, 2012.
———. *The Polysyllabic Spree*. San Francisco: Believer Books, 2004.
———. *Shakespeare Wrote for Money*. San Francisco: Believer Books, 2008.
Hsu, Chun-Ting, Conrad, Markus, and Jacobs, Arthur. "Fiction Feelings in Harry Potter: Haemodynamic Response in the Mid-Cingulate Cortex Correlates with Immersive Reading." *Neuroreport* 25:17 (2014): 1356–61.
Hui, Yuk. *On the Existence of Digital Objects*. Minneapolis: University of Minnesota Press, 2016.
Ingarden, Roman. *The Cognition of the Literary Work of Art*, trans. Ruth Ann Crowley and Kenneth R. Olson. Evanston, IL: Northwestern University Press, 1973.
———. *The Literary Work of Art*, trans. George Grabowicz. Evanston, IL: Northwestern University Press, 1973.
Ingraham, Christopher. "Leisure Reading in the U.S. Is at an All-Time Low." *Washington Post* (29 June 2018). https://www.washingtonpost.com/news/wonk/wp/2018/06/29/leisure-reading-in-the-u-s-is-at-an-all-time-low. Accessed 12 March 2020.
Iser, Wolfgang. *The Act of Reading: A Theory of Aesthetic Response*, trans. David Henry Wilson. Baltimore, MD: Johns Hopkins University Press, 1978.
———. *The Implied Reader: Patterns of Communication in Prose Fiction from Bunyan to Beckett*, trans. David Henry Wilson. Baltimore, MD: Johns Hopkins University Press, 1974.
———. "The Reading Process: A Phenomenological Approach." In *Reader Response Criticism: From Formalism to Post-Structuralism*, ed. Jane Tompkins. Baltimore, MD: Johns Hopkins University Press, 1980, 50–69.
Iser, Wolfgang, Holland, Norman, and Booth, Wayne. "Interview: Wolfgang Iser." *Diacritics* 10:2 (Summer 1980): 57–74.
Jabr, Ferris. "Why the Brain Prefers Paper." *Scientific American* 309:5 (November 2013): 48–53.
Jacobs, Alan. *The Pleasures of Reading in an Age of Distraction*. New York: Oxford University Press, 2011.
James, Henry. *Theory of Fiction*, ed. James Miller. Lincoln: University of Nebraska Press, 1972.
Kidd, David, and Castano, Emanuele. "Reading Literary Fiction Improves Theory of Mind." *Science* 342:6156 (18 October 2013). http://science.sciencemag.org/content/342/6156/377. Accessed 12 July 2017.
Kivy, Peter. *The Performance of Reading: An Essay in the Philosophy of Literature*. Oxford: Blackwell, 2006.
Levinas, Emmanuel. "The Other in Proust." In *The Levinas Reader*, trans. Sean Hand, ed. Seán Hand. Oxford: Blackwell, 1989, 160–65.
———. *Totality and Infinity*, trans. Alphonso Lingis. Pittsburgh, PA: Duquesne University Press, 1969.
Lucian of Samosata. "Remarks Addressed to an Illiterate Book Fancier," trans. H. W. Fowler and F. G. Fowler. http://lucianofsamosata.info/RemarksOfIlliterateBookFancier.html#sthash.rdCnDgi0. Accessed 12 July 2017.
Machiavelli, Niccolo. "Letter to Francesco Vettori, His Benefactor." In *The Prince*, trans. C. E. Detmold. London: Wordsworth, 1997, 128.
MacIntyre, Alasdair. *After Virtue*. 3rd ed. Notre Dame, IN: University of Notre Dame Press, 2007.

———. *A Short History of Ethics*. 2nd. ed. Notre Dame, IN: University of Notre Dame Press, 1998.

———. *Whose Justice? Which Rationality?* Notre Dame, IN: University of Notre Dame Press, 1988.

MacSkimming, Roy. *The Perilous Trade: Publishing Canada's Writers*. Toronto: McLelland and Stewart, 2003.

Marcel, Gabriel. *The Mystery of Being, Volume 1: Reflection and Mystery*, trans. G. S. Fraser. London: Harvill Press, 1951.

McInerney, Jay. "Faking It." *New York Times* (11 November 2007).

McCormick, Thomas. *Theories of Reading in Dialogue: An Interdisciplinary Study*. Lanham, MD: University Press of America, 1988.

McGinn, Colin. *Ethics, Evil and Literature*. Oxford: Clarendon Press, 1997.

McMurtry, Larry. *Books: A Memoir*. New York: Simon and Schuster, 2008.

Mendelson-Maoz, Adia. "Ethics and Literature: Introduction." *Philosophia* 35 (2007): 111–16.

Miller, John Hillis. *The Ethics of Reading: Kant, de Man, Eliot, Trollope, James, and Benjamin*. New York: Columbia University Press, 1987.

Mulhall, Stephen. *On Film*. 2nd ed. London: Routledge, 2008.

Nabokov, Vladimir. *Lectures on Literature*, ed. Fredson Bowers. San Diego: Harvest, 1980.

Nagel, Thomas. *The View from Nowhere*. Oxford: Oxford University Press, 1986.

National Endowment for the Arts. *Reading on the Rise: A New Chapter in American Literacy*. 2009. https://www.arts.gov/sites/default/files/ReadingonRise.pdf. Accessed 12 July 2017.

Nussbaum, Martha. *Creating Capabilities: The Human Development Approach*. Cambridge, MA: Harvard University Press, 2011.

———. *Love's Knowledge*. Oxford: Oxford University Press, 1990.

———. *Poetic Justice*. Boston, MA: Beacon Press, 1995.

Orwell, George. "Bookshop Memories." In *An Age Like This: The Collected Essays, Journalism and Letters of George Orwell, Volume 1*, ed. Sonia Orwell and Ian Angus. London: Secker and Warburg, 1968, 242–47.

Parini, Jay. "The Considerable Satisfaction of Two Pages a Day." *Chronicle of Higher Education* (8 April 2005).

Paul, Pamela. "My Life with Bob." *New York Times* (13 April 2012).

Piercey, Robert. "Not Choosing between Morality and Ethics." *Philosophical Forum* 32:1 (March 2001): 53–72.

———. *The Uses of the Past from Heidegger to Rorty: Doing Philosophy History*. Cambridge: Cambridge University Press, 2009.

Piper, Andrew. *Book Was There: Reading in Electronic Times*. Chicago: University of Chicago Press, 2012.

———. "Out of Touch: E-Reading Isn't Reading." *Slate* (15 November 2012). http://www.slate.com/articles/arts/culturebox/2012/11/reading_on_a_kindle_is_not_the_same_as_reading_a_book.html. Accessed 12 July 2017.

Pippin, Robert. *After the Beautiful: Hegel and the Philosophy of Pictorial Modernism*. Chicago: University of Chicago Press, 2014.

Poulet, Georges. "Criticism and the Experience of Interiority." In *Reader Response Criticism: From Formalism to Post-Structuralism*, ed. Jane Tompkins. Baltimore, MD: Johns Hopkins University Press, 1980, 41–49.

Powers, William. *Hamlet's Blackberry: A Practical Philosophy for Building a Good Life in the Digital Age*. New York: HarperCollins, 2010.

Proust, Marcel. "On Reading." In *Reading in Bed*, trans. Jean Autret and William Buford, ed. Steven Gilbar (Boston, MA: David Godine: 1995), 39–44.
Pyne, Lydia. *Bookshelf*. London: Bloomsbury, 2016.
Queenan, Joe. *One for the Books*. New York: Viking, 2012.
Reagan, Charles. *Paul Ricoeur: His Life and Work*. Chicago: University of Chicago Press, 1996.
Ricoeur, Paul. "The Hermeneutical Function of Distanciation." In *From Text to Action*, trans. Kathleen Blamey and John Thompson. Evanston, IL: Northwestern University Press, 1991, 75–88.
———. "Hermeneutics and the Critique of Ideology." In *From Text to Action*, trans. Kathleen Blamey and John Thompson. Evanston, IL: Northwestern University Press, 1991, 270–307.
———. "The Model of the Text: Meaningful Action Considered as a Text." in *From Text to Action*, trans. Kathleen Blamey and John Thompson. Evanston, IL: Northwestern University Press, 1991, 144–67.
———. *Oneself as Another*, trans. Kathleen Blamey. Chicago: University of Chicago Press, 1991.
———. *Time and Narrative*, Volume 1, trans. Kathleen McLaughlin and David Pellauer. Chicago: University of Chicago Press, 1984.
———. *Time and Narrative*, Volume 3, trans. Kathleen McLaughlin and David Pellauer (Chicago: University of Chicago Press, 1988), 101.
Ridley, Aaron. *Philosophy of Music: Theme and Variations*. Edinburgh: Edinburgh University Press, 2004.
Rorty, Richard. *Contingency, Irony, and Solidarity*. Cambridge: Cambridge University Press, 1989.
———. "The Historiography of Philosophy: Four Genres." In *Truth and Progress: Philosophical Papers, Volume* 3 (Cambridge: Cambridge University Press, 1998, 247–73.
———. "Philosophy as a Transitional Genre." In *The Rorty Reader*, ed. Christopher Voparil and Richard Bernstein. Oxford: Wiley-Blackwell, 2010, 473–88.
———. "Trotsky and the Wild Orchids." In *The Rorty Reader*, ed. Christopher Voparil and Richard Bernstein. Oxford: Wiley-Blackwell, 2010, 500–510.
———. "Twenty-Five Years After." In *The Rorty Reader*, ed. Christopher Voparil and Richard Bernstein. Oxford: Wiley-Blackwell, 2010, 175–79.
Rorty, Richard, Schneewind, Jerome, and Skinner, Quentin. "Introduction." In *Philosophy in History*, ed. Richard Rorty, Jerome Schneewind and Quentin Skinner. Cambridge: Cambridge University Press, 1984, 1–14.
Russon, John. "Reading: Derrida in Hegel's Understanding." *Research in Phenomenology* 36 (2006): 181–200.
Stow, Simon. "Reading Our Way to Democracy? Literature and Public Ethics." *Philosophy and Literature* 30:2 (2006): 410–23.
———. *Republic of Readers? The Literary Turn in Political Thought and Analysis* (Albany: SUNY Press, 2008).
Saenger, Paul. *Space between Words: The Origins of Silent Reading*. Stanford, CA: Stanford University Press, 2000.
Sartre, Jean-Paul. *Nausea*, trans. Lloyd Alexander. New York: New Directions, 1964.
Sax, David. *The Revenge of Analog: Real Things and Why They Matter*. New York: Public Affairs, 2016.
Schopenhauer, Arthur. "On Books and Writing." In *Essays and Aphorisms*, trans. R. J. Hollingdale. London: Penguin, 1970, 198–211.

Schwartz, Lynne. *Ruined by Reading: A Life in Books*. Boston, MA: Beacon Press, 1996.

Sen, Amartya. *Commodities and Capabilities*. Amsterdam: North Holland, 1985.

Shirky, Clay. *Cognitive Surplus: How Technology Makes Consumers into Collaborators*. London: Penguin, 2010.

Slote, Michael. *Goods and Virtues*. Oxford: Clarendon Press, 1983.

Smith, Debra White. *What Jane Austen Taught Me about Love and Romance*. New York: Harvest House, 2007.

Spacks, Patricia Meyer. *On Rereading*. Cambridge, MA: Harvard University Press, 2011.

Spufford, Francis. *The Child That Books Built*. London: Picador, 2003.

Stetka, Brad. "Why Everyone Should Read *Harry Potter*." *Scientific American* (9 September 2014). http://www.scientificamerican.com/article/why-everyone-should-read-harry-potter. Accessed 12 July 2017.

Süskind, Patrick. "Amnesia in Litteris: The Books I Have Read (I Think)." *Harper's Magazine* (March 1987): 71–73.

Svenbro, Jesper. "Archaic and Classical Greece: The Invention of Silent Reading." In *A History of Reading in the* West, ed. Guglielmo Cavallo and Roger Chartier, trans. Lydia Cochrane. Amherst: University of Massachusetts Press, 1999, 37–63.

Taylor, Mark. "The Impact of Reading on Career Prospects." *Books for Keeps* 189 (2011). http://booksforkeeps.co.uk/member/mark-taylor. Accessed 12 July 2017.

Weiss, Philip. "The Book Thief: A True Tale of Bibliomania." *Harper's Magazine* (January 1994): 37–56.

Wolf, Maryanne. *Proust and the Squid: The Story and Science of the Reading Brain*. New York: HarperCollins, 2007.

Woolf, Virginia. *The Common Reader: First Series*, ed. Andrew McNeillie. New York: Harcourt, 1984.

———. "How Should One Read a Book?." In *The Second Common Reader*. New York: Harcourt, 1932, 258–70.

Worth, Sarah. *In Defense of Reading*. London: Rowman and Littlefield, 2017.

INDEX

Act of Reading, The (Iser) 19
Adler, Mortimer 57–60, 76
alterior approach, reading 63–65
American Psycho 55

Banks, Iain M. 31
Baron, Naomi 93
Basbane, Nicholas 2
Baudrillard, Jean 76
Bayard, Pierre 2, 12, 29, 81–87
Benjamin, Walter 5, 74–76, 88–90
Benton, Michael 6
bibliomania 76
Bloom, Harold 2, 4, 33, 41–42
Blumberg, Stephen 77
books 74–81
Books: A Memoir (McMurtry) 2
"Bookshop Memories" (Orwell) 74
Booth, Wayne 41, 63
Brooklyn (Toibin) 33
Bruns, Gerald 51–52
Burden, Carter 76–77

Carr, Nicholas 93
Cavell, Stanley 16–18
Child That Books Built, The (Spufford) 2
Citizen Vince 29, 31
Clockwork Orange, A 42
collectors, collection of 88–90
"Common Reader, The" (Woolf) 8–10
common readers 8–10
Company We Keep, The (Booth) 41
consistency-building 20
Contingency, Irony, and Solidarity (Rorty) 41
conversational approach, reading 47–49
Critique of Judgment (Kant) 78–79
Currie, Gregory 42, 53

deontological approach, reading 61–63
Dickens, Charles 36, 48–49

e-books 92–93
Eco, Umberto 82
Edmundson, Mark 2
Eliot, T. S. 32
Elliot, George 63
ethics from reading 5, 41–56
    benefits 53–56
    conversational approach 47–49
    hermeneutical approach 49–53
    improvement 41–43
    supply-side approach 43–47
ethics of reading 5, 57–69
    alterior approach 63–65
    deontological approach 61–63
    eudaimonistic approach 65–67
    history 67–69
    practices 67–69
    responsibilities 59–61
    responsible readers 57–59
    traditions 67–69
eudaimonistic approach, reading 65–67
Excession (Banks) 31
Ex Libris (Fadiman) 15

Fadiman, Anne 15, 23, 61–62
feelings, reader 34–36
Fforde, Jasper 15
fiction feeling hypothesis 17–18
Fifty Shades of Grey 93
Foucault's Pendulum (Eco) 82
Franny and Zooey 34, 36
Franzen, Jonathan 2, 6
Freire, Paulo 1

Gadamer, Hans-Georg 21–22, 46–47, 50–52
Gestalt 20–21, 23
Gibson, Andrew 41
Gilkey, John 77
Grisham, John 31

Hamlet (Shakespeare) 32, 51–52, 55, 83
Hard Times 46, 48–49, 52
Harry Potter 41
Hart, Michael 92
Hazlitt, William 32
Heidegger, Martin 24–25, 50, 74, 86
hermeneutical approach, reading 49–53
Hornby, Nick 27–39, 42
  feeling as reader 34–36
  life as reader 27–39
  quests 36–39
  reading 27–39
  rereading 32–34
  stories 36–39
How Proust Can Change Your Life (de Botton) 2
"How Should One Read a Book?" (Woolf) 60
How to Read a Book (Adler) 57, 60
How to Read and Why (Bloom) 2
How to Read Literature Like a Professor (Foster) 2
How to Talk about Books You Haven't Read (Bayard) 12, 81, 84–85
human rights 61
Husserl, Edmund 18, 50

implied author 63
Implied Reader, The (Iser) 19
Ingarden, Roman 18
inner books 82–84
In Search of Lost Time (Proust) 38–39
Iser, Wolfgang 18–24

Jabr, Ferris 93
Jacobs, Alan 4, 18, 57–58, 79
James, Henry 16–18
Jane Eyre (Fforde) 15
Johnson, Samuel 8
JurisFiction 15

Kivy, Peter 78, 85

Levinas, Emmanuel 18, 24, 63

MacIntyre, Alasdair 11, 38, 58, 66–69, 94–97
Madame Bovary 72, 77–78, 85, 98
Man Who Loved Books Too Much, The (Bartlett) 2
Marcel, Gabriel 74
Marry Me 29–30
McGahern, John 15
McGinn, Colin 41
McInerney, Jay 85
Mein Kampf 55
mimesis$_2$/configuration 52
mimesis$_1$/prefiguration 52–53
mimesis$_3$/refiguration 52–53
Moby Dick 12
"Model of the Text, The" (Ricoeur) 50–51
Mulhall, Stephen 3

Nagel, Thomas 86
Native Son (Wright) 46, 52
Nausea (Sartre) 75
Nussbaum, Martha 43–46, 50–51, 53–55, 62

Old School (Wolff) 34
"On Reading Old Books" (Hazlitt) 32
ontology of reading 5, 71–90
  books 74–81
  collectors, collection of 88–90
  virtual collection 81–85
  writ large collection 85–87
Orwell, George 23, 74–76, 80

Parini, Jay 47
Patience and Fortitude (Basbanes) 2
Paul, Pamela 78
Phaedrus (Plato) 7
phantom books 82–84
philosophy 3
  changes 99–103
  history of 7–8
  of reading 3–7
    ethics 5, 41–69
    ontology 5, 71–90
    selfhood 4, 15–26
Pickwick Papers, The (Dickens) 48–49

INDEX

Piper, Andrew 6–7, 93, 98
Poetic Justice (Nussbaum) 43–45
Poetics (Aristotle) 82
Proust, Marcel 16–18, 31, 38–39, 82
Proust and the Squid 2

Queenan, Joe 77

readers 6–7
  common 8–10
  digital future 91–92
  existence 51–52
  experiences of 10–14, 16–26
  feeling 34–36
  Hornby's story as 28–39
  philosophy 99–103
  practices 92–96
  responsibilities 57–59
    alterior approach 63–65
    deontological view of 61–63
    eudaimonistic approach 65–67
  sense of isolation 15–26
  traditions 96–99
  what to read and 29–32
  world 50
reading 1–3, 7–8
  act of 19–22
  benefits 1–2
  as consistent interpretation 22–24
  of continuous presentness 16
  ethics from 5, 41–56
  ethics of 5, 57–69
  experiences 10–14, 16–26
  improvement 41–43
  Iser's phenomenology of 19–24
  life 27–39
  ontology 71–90
  people care about 1–2
  as philosophical activity 3–7
  as practices 11–13, 25–26
    advantage 11–12
    mutable 11
    social 11
    structured 11
  private activity 5–6
  revelation and 50
  self 15–26
  sense 41
  things 71–90
  transformation and 50
  what to read 29–32
Reading in the Brain (Dehaene) 2
reading things 71–90
  books 74–81
  collectors, collection of 88–90
  virtual collection 81–85
rereading 32–34
revelation 50
Ricoeur, Paul 43, 49–55
Ridley, Aaron 24–25
Robinson, Marilynne 29
Rorty, Richard 4, 41
Rowling, J. K. 41
Ruined by Reading (Schwartz) 2
Russon, John 7

Salinger, J. D. 30
Sartre, Jean-Paul 75
Schwartz, Lynne 2
screen books 82–83
selfhood 4, 15–26
self reading 15–26
  act 19–22
  Iser's phenomenology of 19–24
Sen, Amartya 54–55
Shallows, The (Carr) 93
Shirky, Clay 92–93
Slote, Michael 37–38
Smith, Adam 44–45
Splendor of Letters, A (Basbanes) 2
Stow, Simon 46–48, 50–53
Stuff I've Been Reading 27–31, 34–38
supply-side approach, reading 43–47

Time and Narrative (Ricoeur) 49
Toibin, Colm 33
transformation 50
Tristram Shandy 25

Ulysses 25
"Unpacking My Library" (Benjamin) 74, 80, 88–90

virtual collection 81–85

Walter, Jess 29
War and Peace 42

What Jane Austen Taught Me about Love and Romance (Smith) 2
what to read 29–32
Why You Should Read Kafka before You Waste Your Life (Hawes) 2

Wolff, Tobias 34
Wood, James 33
Woolf, Virginia 8–10, 23, 25, 60, 67–68, 90
world 50
Wright, Richard 46, 48

www.ingramcontent.com/pod-product-compliance
Lightning Source LLC
Chambersburg PA
CBHW021833300426
44114CB00009BA/424